Handwriting Today

This book belongs to

....

The cursive handwriting programme

HELEN WOODS

Prim-Ed Publishing

Handwriting Today Book A
Published by Prim-Ed Publishing
Republic of Ireland and the UK:
Marshmeadows, New Ross, Co. Wexford

© R.I.C. Publications
Republished by Prim-Ed Publishing 2010
ISBN 978-1-84654-232-9

Copyright Notice
No part of this book may be reproduced in any form or by any means, electronic or mechanical, including photocopying or recording, or by any information storage or retrieval system without written permission from the publisher.

Foreword

Handwriting Today provides teachers with a systematic approach to the instruction and practice of cursive handwriting. The font used – Peannaireacht – has been developed to provide a cursive manuscript font that combines the best of traditional and contemporary handwriting practice. The series has been written in the belief that it is essential for all children to develop fluent, legible and attractive handwriting.

This handwriting programme develops:
- muscular coordination;
- fine motor skills;
- a preferred writing hand;
- a comfortable and appropriate pencil grip;
- a comfortable and appropriate posture when writing;
- a positive attitude toward handwriting;
- an ability to complete patterns which develop the movement and process of handwriting;
- a visual memory of letter shapes and formations;
- a fluent, legible and attractive writing style; and
- the ability to follow instructions.

Each double page develops the correct formation of the particular letter being treated, and follows the same format, so children are able to concentrate on the process of handwriting. The progressive development of each double page ensures children practise:

- the correct movement associated with the letter;
- the correct technique for writing the letter;
- the correct formation of the letter; and
- flow and fluency in writing the letter.

Letters have been grouped according to the direction the letter is formed.

Review pages have been included at regular intervals to allow teachers to assess each child's handwriting.

The cursive font used in **Handwriting Today** is Peannaireacht cursive which has been developed in Ireland for use in Irish schools.

Contents

Prewriting Activities	2 – 5
Anticlockwise Letters	
Aa (ambulance)	6 – 7
Cc (caterpillar)	8 – 9
Dd (dinosaur)	10 – 11
Ee (eggs)	12 – 13
Ff (flowers)	14 – 15
Gg (grapes)	16 – 17
Oo (octopus)	18 – 19
Qq (queen)	20 – 21
Review anticlockwise letters	22 – 23
Clockwise Letters	
Ss (snake)	24 – 25
Hh (hand)	26 – 27
Kk (kettle)	28 – 29
Mm (mouse)	30 – 31
Nn (necklace)	32 – 33
Pp (peacock)	34 – 35
Rr (rabbit)	36 – 37
Xx (xylophone)	38 – 39
Zz (zigzag)	40 – 41
Review clockwise letters	42 – 43
Downstroke Letters	
Bb (bird)	44 – 45
Ii (ice-cream)	46 – 47
Jj (jeans)	48 – 49
Ll (ladder)	50 – 51
Tt (towel)	52 – 53
Uu (umbrella)	54 – 55
Vv (vase)	56 – 57
Ww (wheelbarrow)	58 – 59
Yy (yacht)	60 – 61
Review downstroke letters	62 – 63
Numbers	
0	64
1	65
2	66
3	67
4	68
5	69
6	70
7	71
8	72
9	73
Review of numbers	74 – 75
Blank writing pages	76 – 77
Assessment	78

Help these animals to reach their food.

Help the bee find the honey.

Help the hen find her eggs.

Handwriting Today

Prim-Ed Publishing – www.prim-ed.com

Trace these patterns.

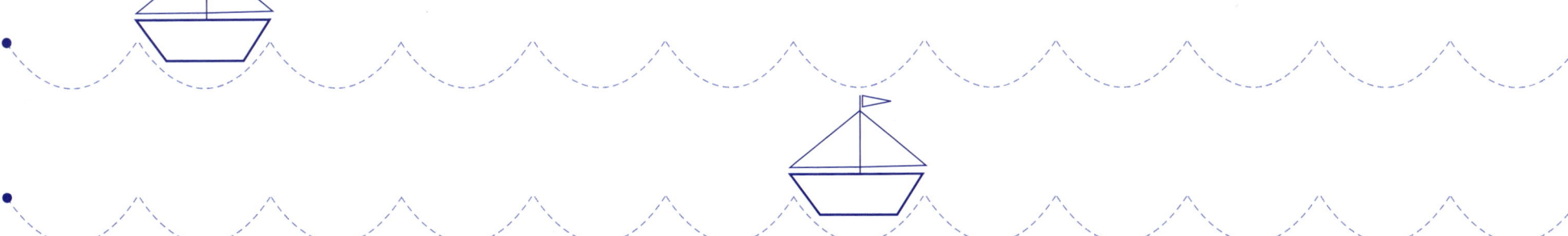

Finish the snails.

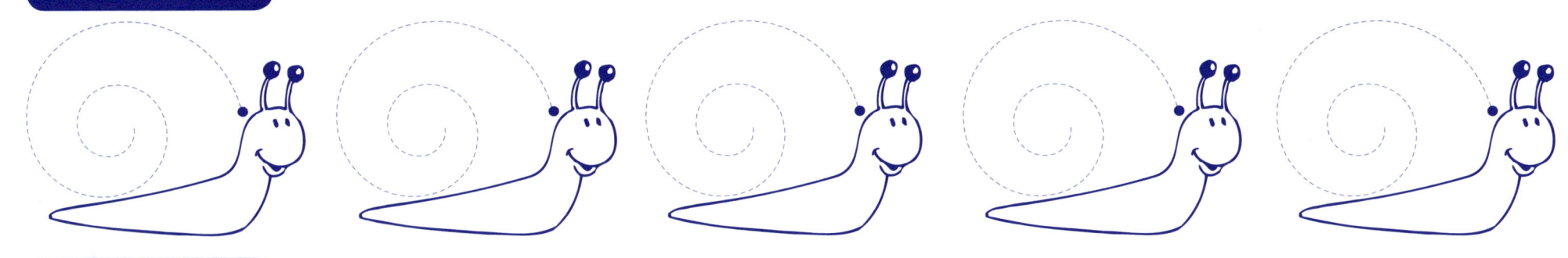

Finish the ice-creams.

Handwriting Today

Prim-Ed Publishing – www.prim-ed.com

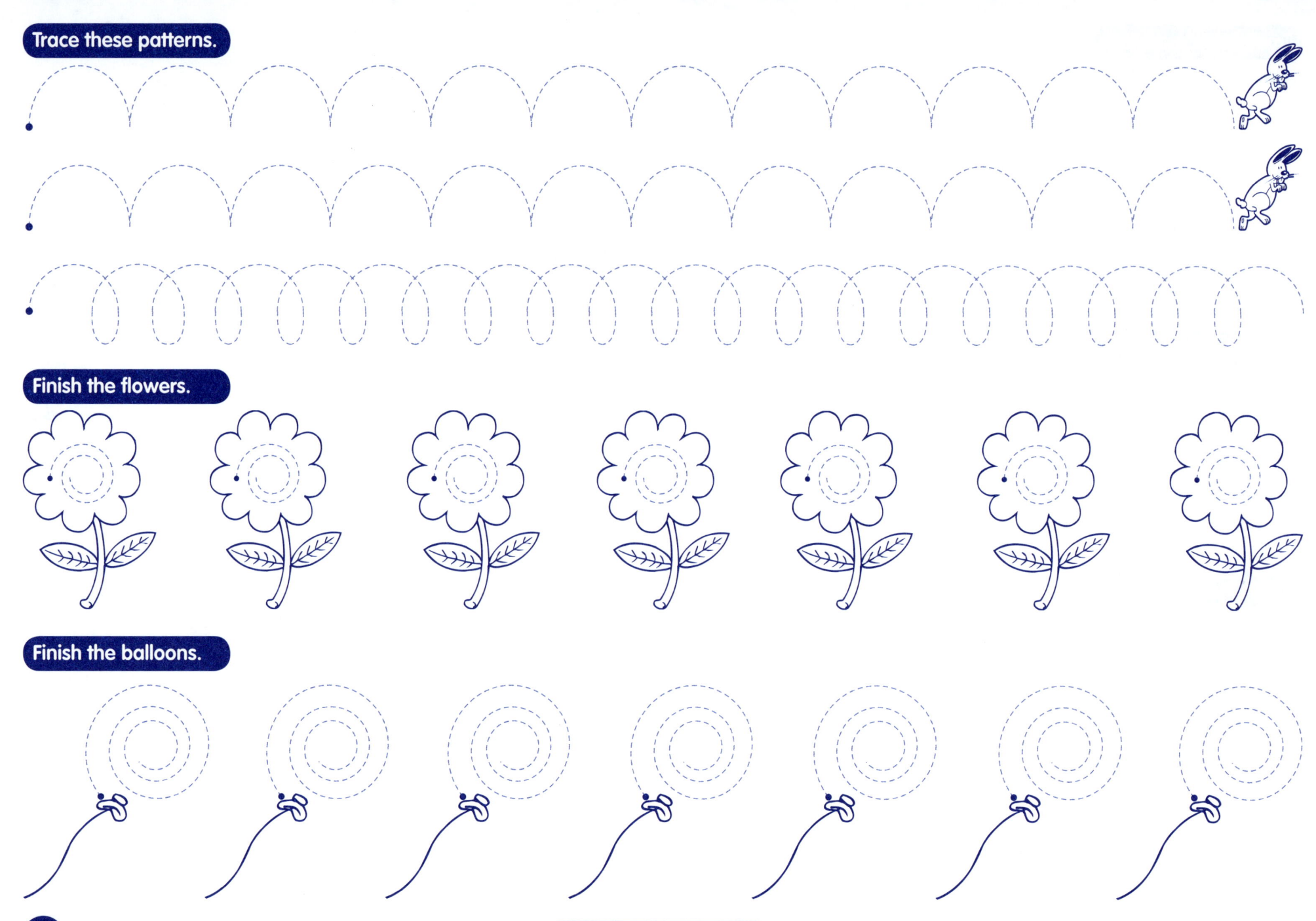

Trace these patterns.

Finish the flowers.

Finish the balloons.

4

Handwriting Today

Prim-Ed Publishing – www.prim-ed.com

Trace this pattern.

Finish the pencils.

Finish the faces.

Finish the candles.

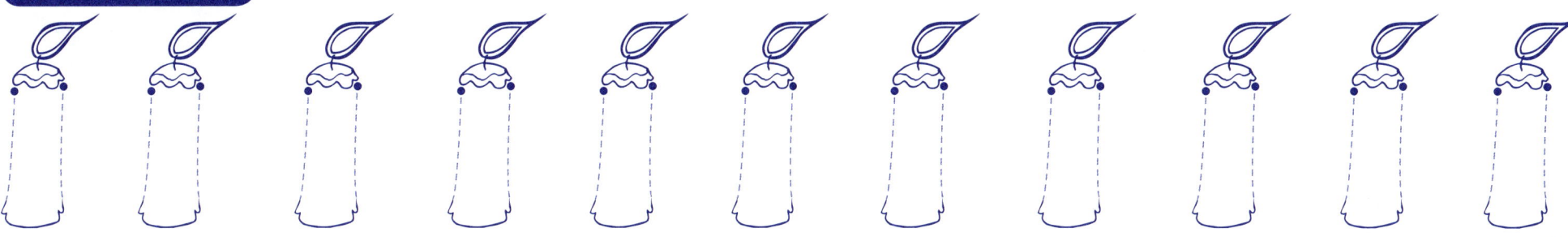

Handwriting Today

A body letter

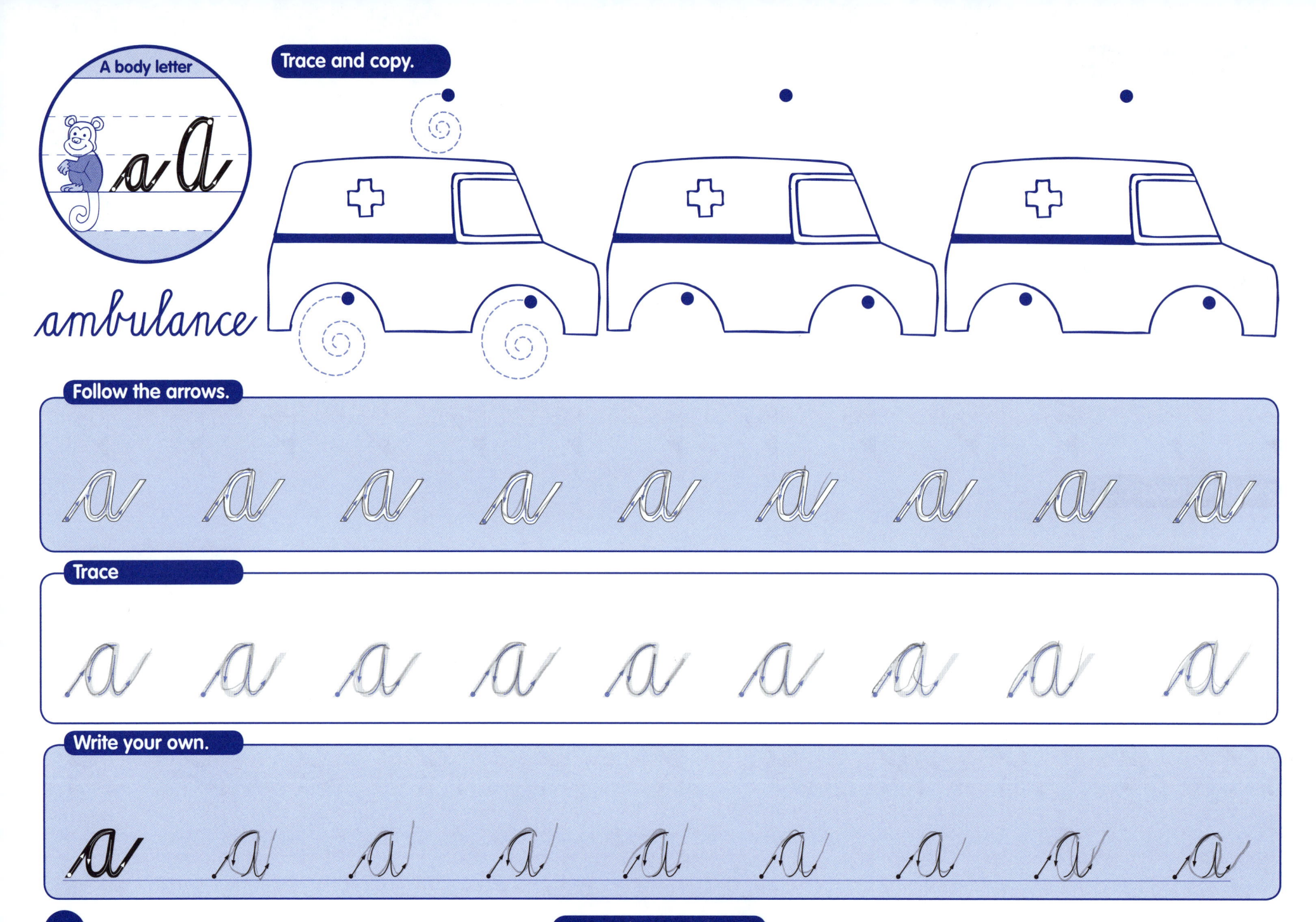

a A

ambulance

Trace and copy.

Follow the arrows.

Trace

Write your own.

6

Handwriting Today

Prim-Ed Publishing – www.prim-ed.com

Trace

uw uw uw uw uw uw uw uw

and at are away an all a

Trace

a a a a a

Trace

a a a a a a

Write your own.

a

Write your own.

a a a a a a

Have a go.

Have a go.

Prim-Ed Publishing – www.prim-ed.com

Handwriting Today

7

A body letter

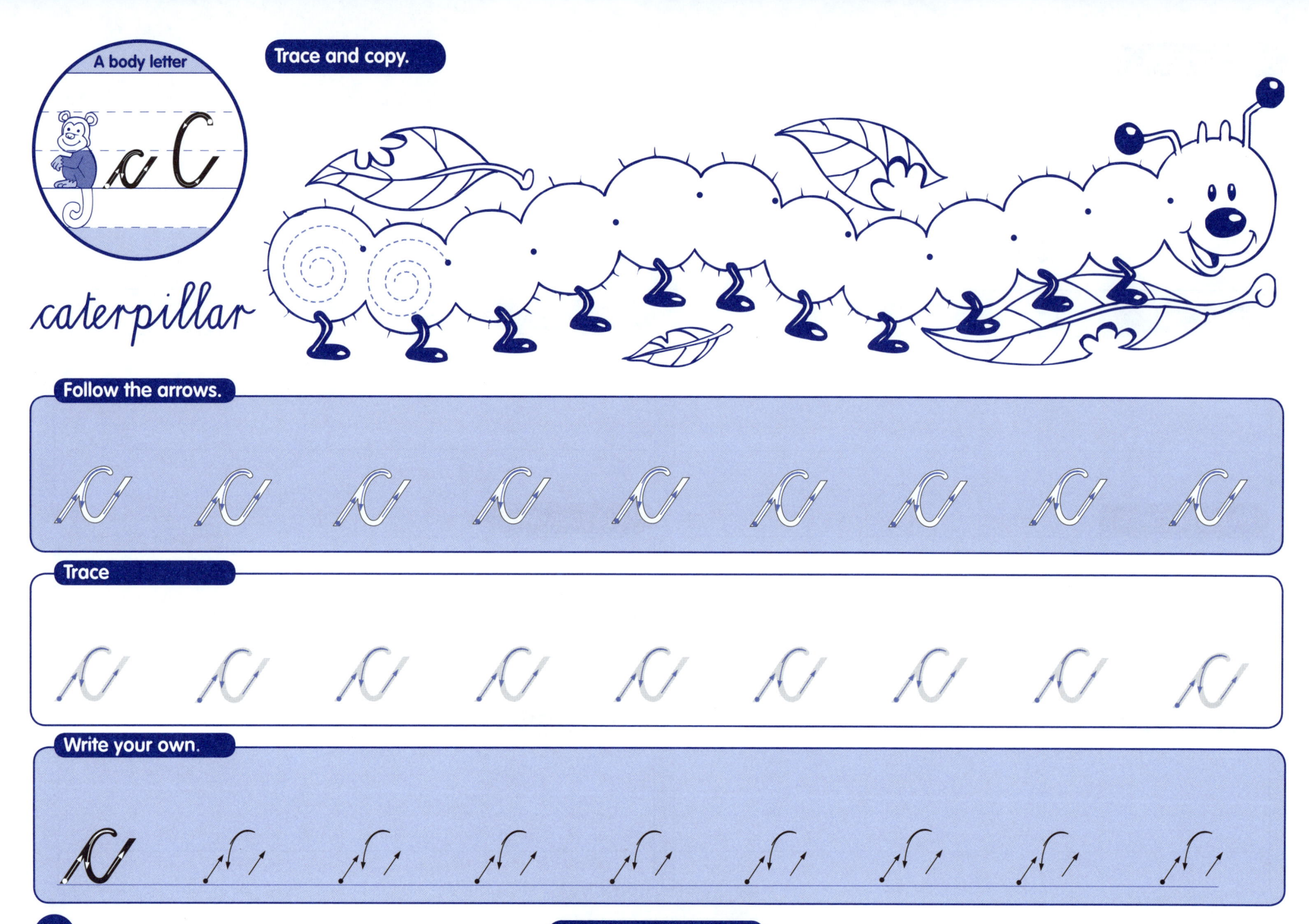

Trace and copy.

caterpillar

Follow the arrows.

Trace

Write your own.

8

Handwriting Today

Prim-Ed Publishing – www.prim-ed.com

Trace

eeee eeee eeee eeee eeee

cat   call   can   came   come   could

Trace

c c c c c c c

Trace

C C C C C C C

Write your own.

c

Write your own.

C

Have a go.

Have a go.

Handwriting Today

Prim-Ed Publishing – www.prim-ed.com

A head and body letter

Trace and copy.

d D

dinosaur

Follow the arrows.

d d d d d d d d d

Trace

d d d d d d d d d

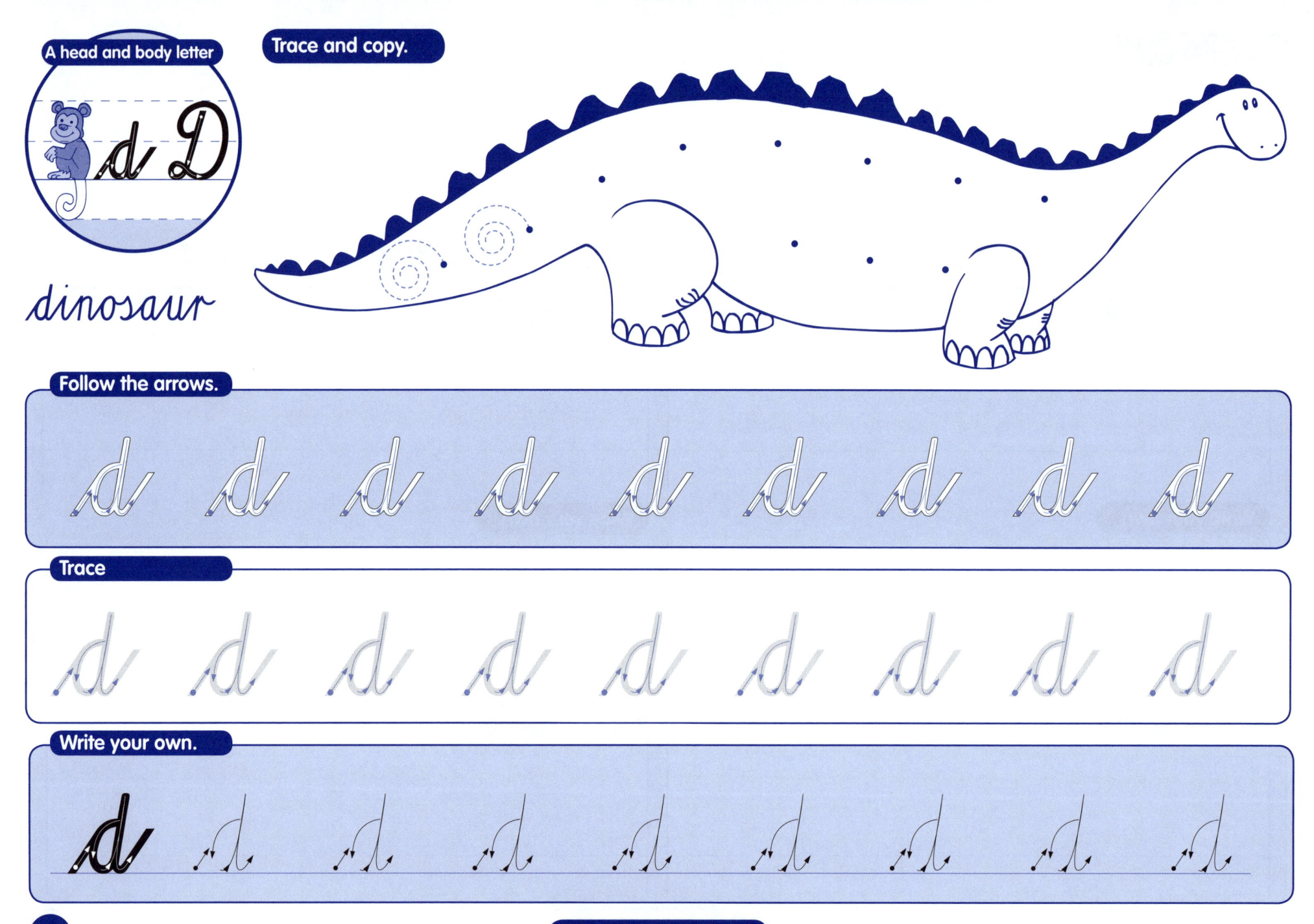

Write your own.

d d d d d d d d d

10   Handwriting Today   Prim-Ed Publishing – www.prim-ed.com

Trace

d d d d d d d d d d

do   did   dog   does   dad   day

Trace

d d d d d d

Trace

D D D D D D

Write your own.

d

Write your own.

D

Have a go.

Have a go.

Handwriting Today

11

A body letter

eggs

Trace and copy.

Follow the arrows.

Trace

Write your own.

12

Handwriting Today

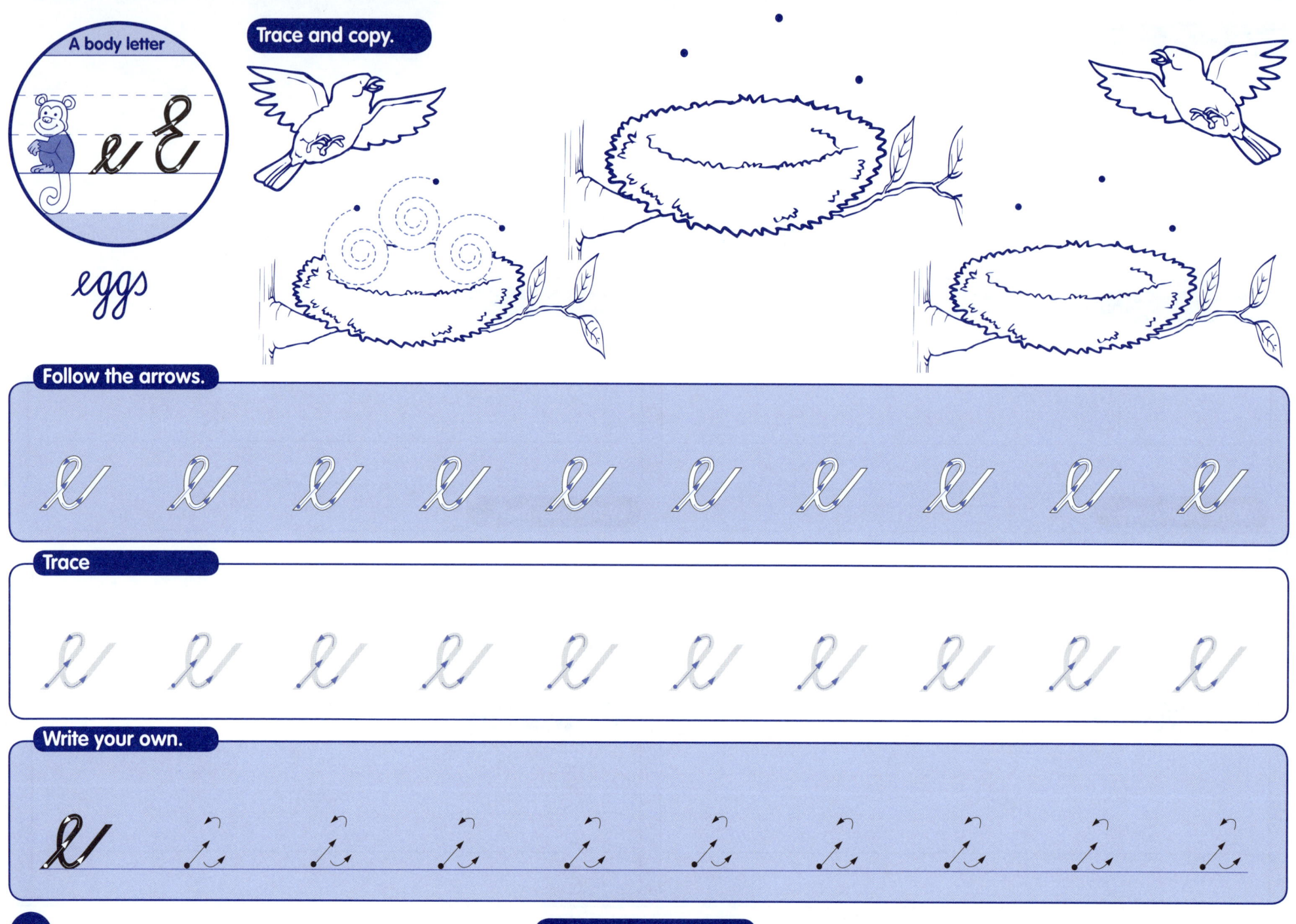

Prim-Ed Publishing – www.prim-ed.com

Trace

eeee eeee eeee eeee eeee eeee

eye   ear   easy   extra   east   every

Trace

e e e e e e e

Trace

E E E E E E E

Write your own.

e

Write your own.

E

Have a go.

Have a go.

Handwriting Today

A head, body and tail letter

flowers

Trace and copy.

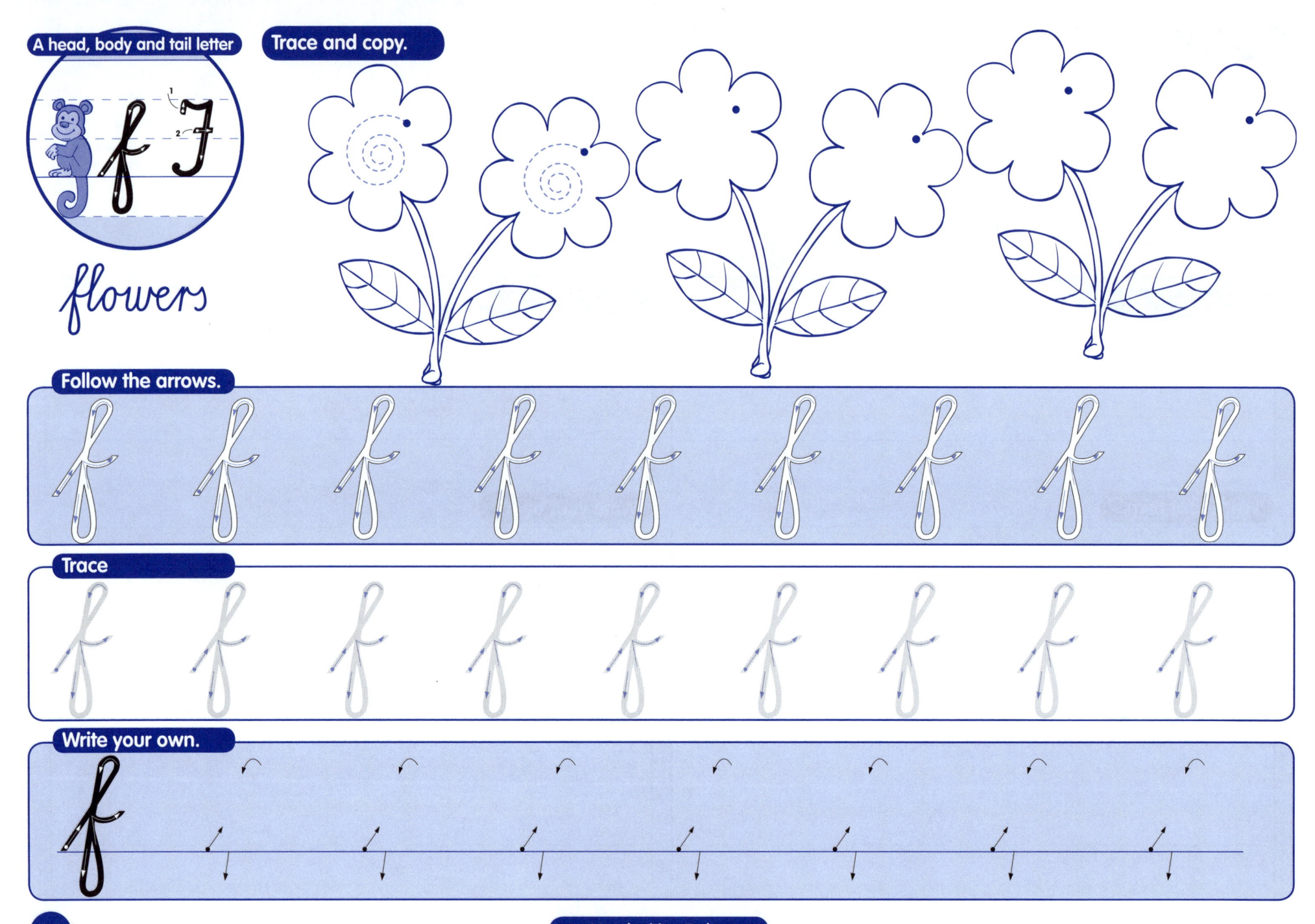

Follow the arrows.

Trace

Write your own.

14

Handwriting Today

Prim-Ed Publishing – www.prim-ed.com

Trace

for   fun   face   from   four   first

Trace

Write your own.

Have a go.

Trace

Write your own.

Have a go.

Handwriting Today

Prim-Ed Publishing – www.prim-ed.com

A body and tail letter

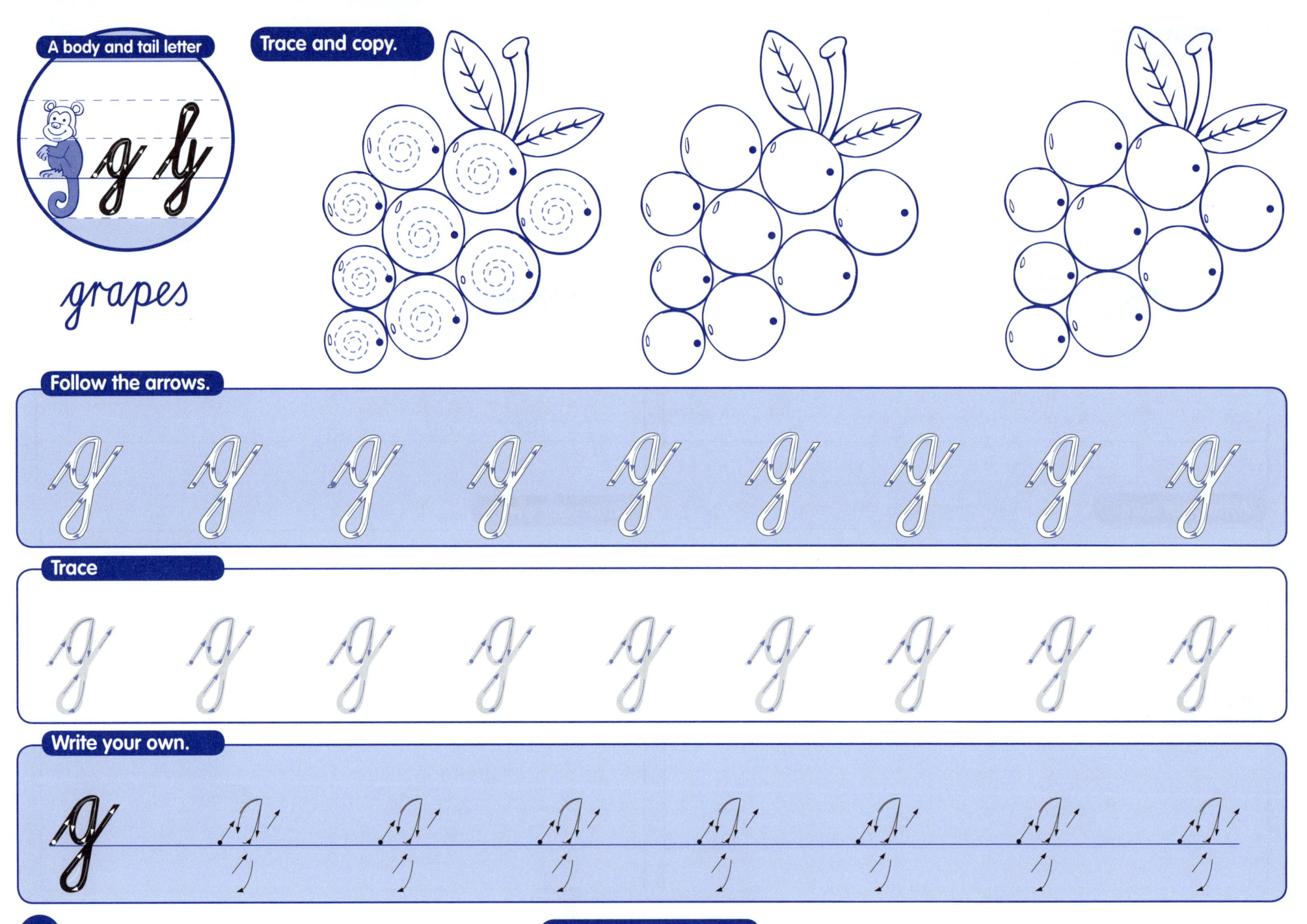

g g

grapes

Trace and copy.

Follow the arrows.

Trace

Write your own.

16 — Handwriting Today — Prim-Ed Publishing – www.prim-ed.com

Trace

go   good   get   got   going   girl

Trace

g g g g g g g g

Trace

gy gy gy gy gy gy gy

Write your own.

g

Write your own.

gy

Have a go

Have a go.

A body letter

o O

octopus

Trace and copy.

Follow the arrows.

Trace

Write your own.

18

Handwriting Today

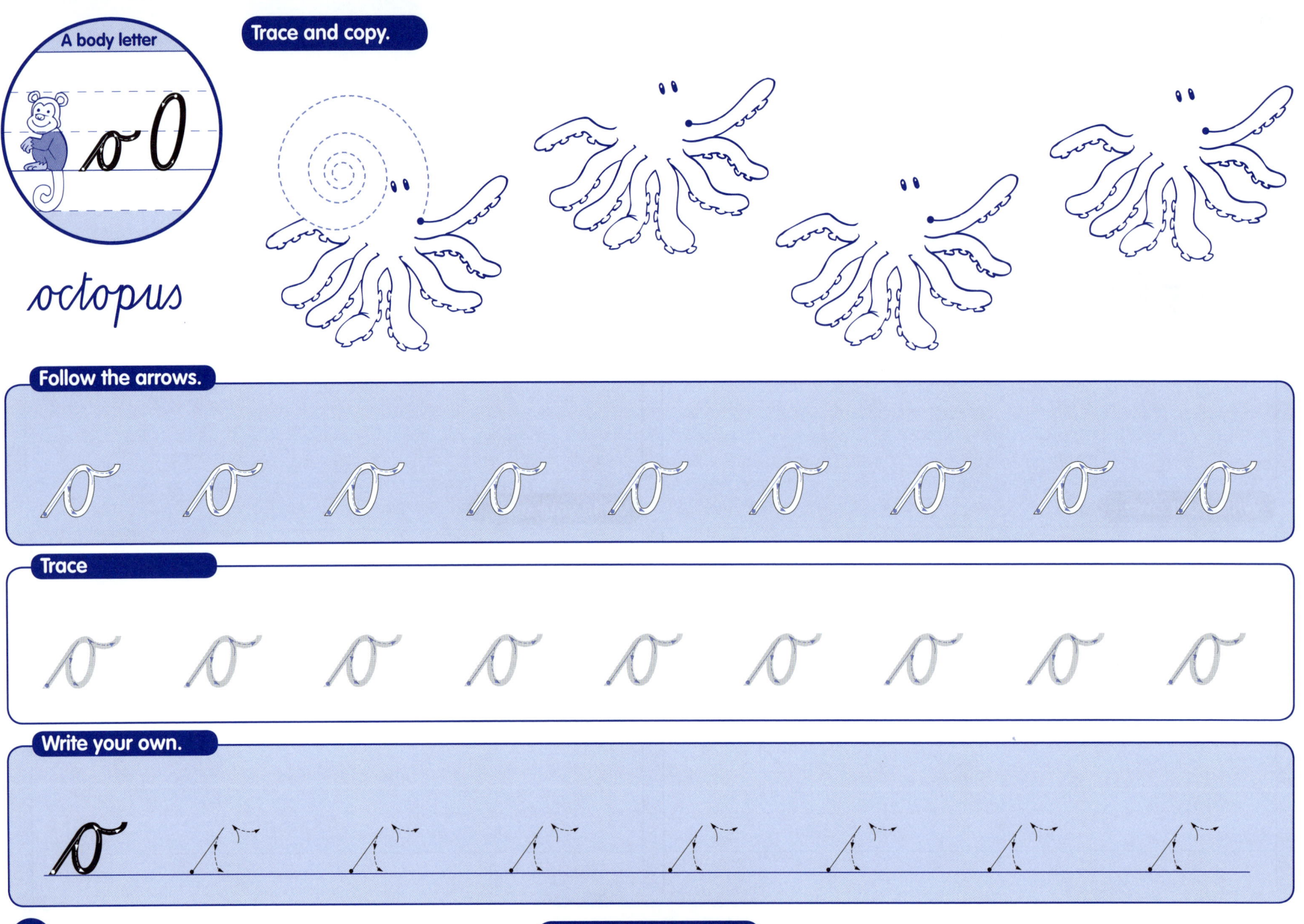

Prim-Ed Publishing – www.prim-ed.com

Trace

oo oo oo oo oo oo

on   off   old   of   one   once

Trace

o o o o o o

Trace

O O O O O O

Write your own.

o

Write your own.

O

Have a go.

Have a go.

Handwriting Today

19

A body and tail letter

q Q

queen

Trace and copy.

Follow the arrows.

Trace

Write your own.

20

Handwriting Today

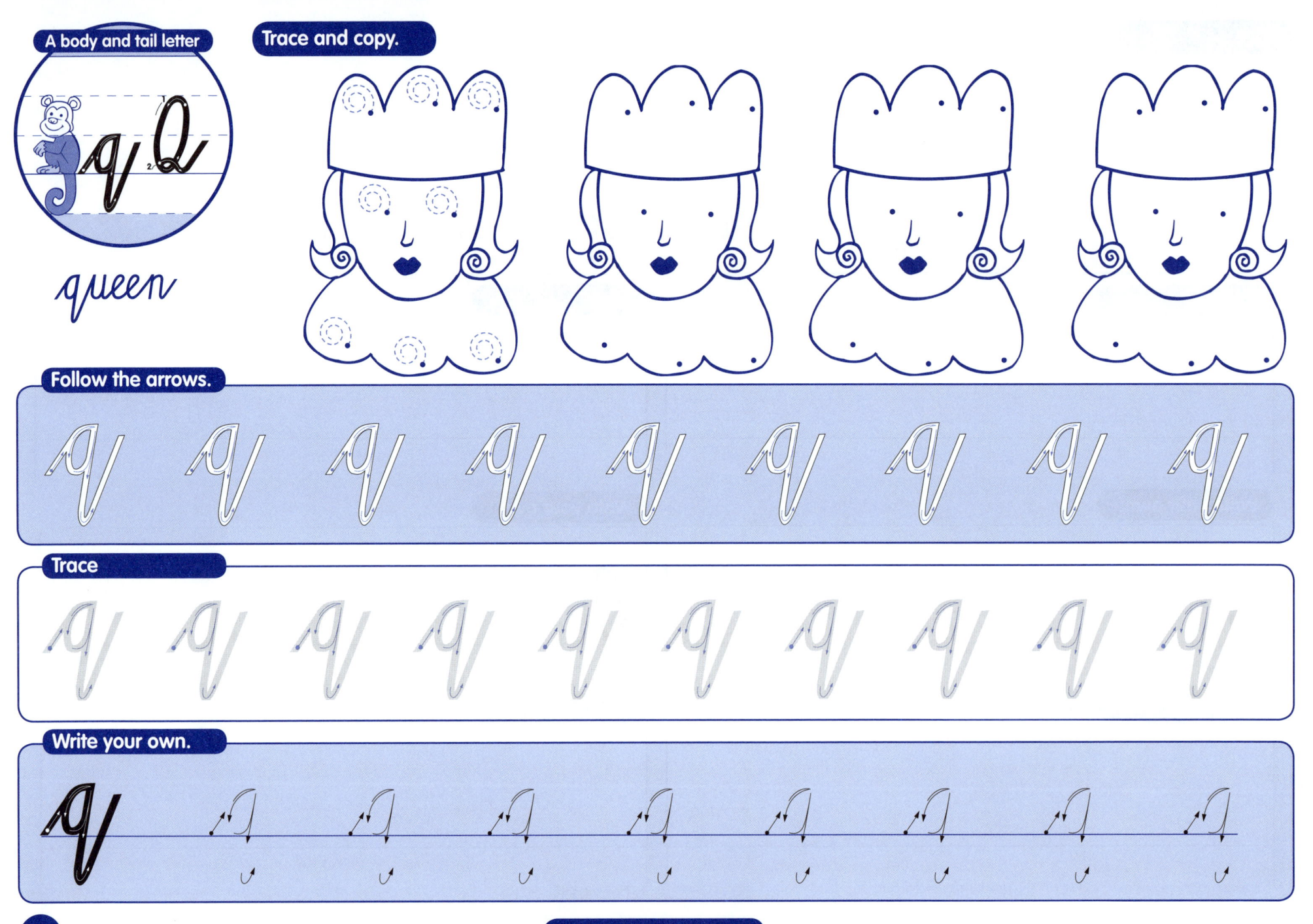

Prim-Ed Publishing – www.prim-ed.com

Trace

quiet   quick   question   queue   quit   quilt

Trace

Trace

Write your own.

Write your own.

Have a go.

Have a go.

Review: a c d e f g o q

Trace

Trace and copy.

a c d e f g o q

Write your own.

22 Handwriting Today

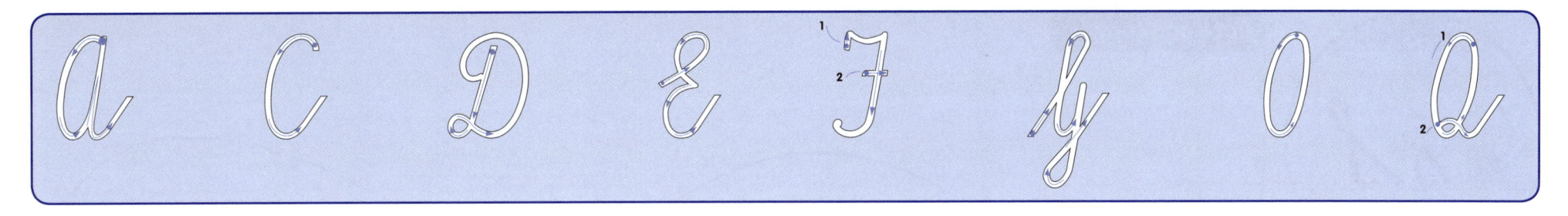

a C D E F G O Q

Trace and copy.

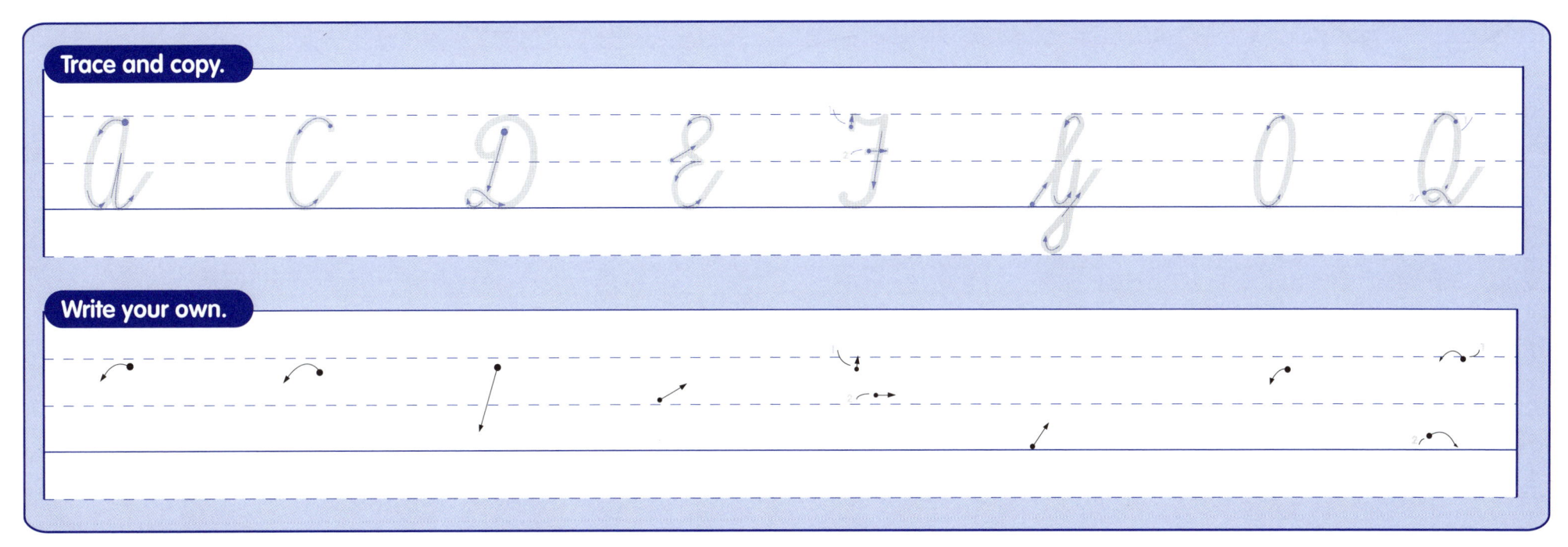

a C D E F G O Q

Write your own.

Assessment

	Demonstrated	Needs further opportunity
Uses a sharp pencil.		
Sits tall with both feet on the floor.		
Holds pencil correctly.		
Forms lower case downstroke letters correctly.		

	Demonstrated	Needs further opportunity
Forms upper case letters correctly.		
Writes neatly and legibly.		
Writes on the lines provided.		

General Comment

A body letter

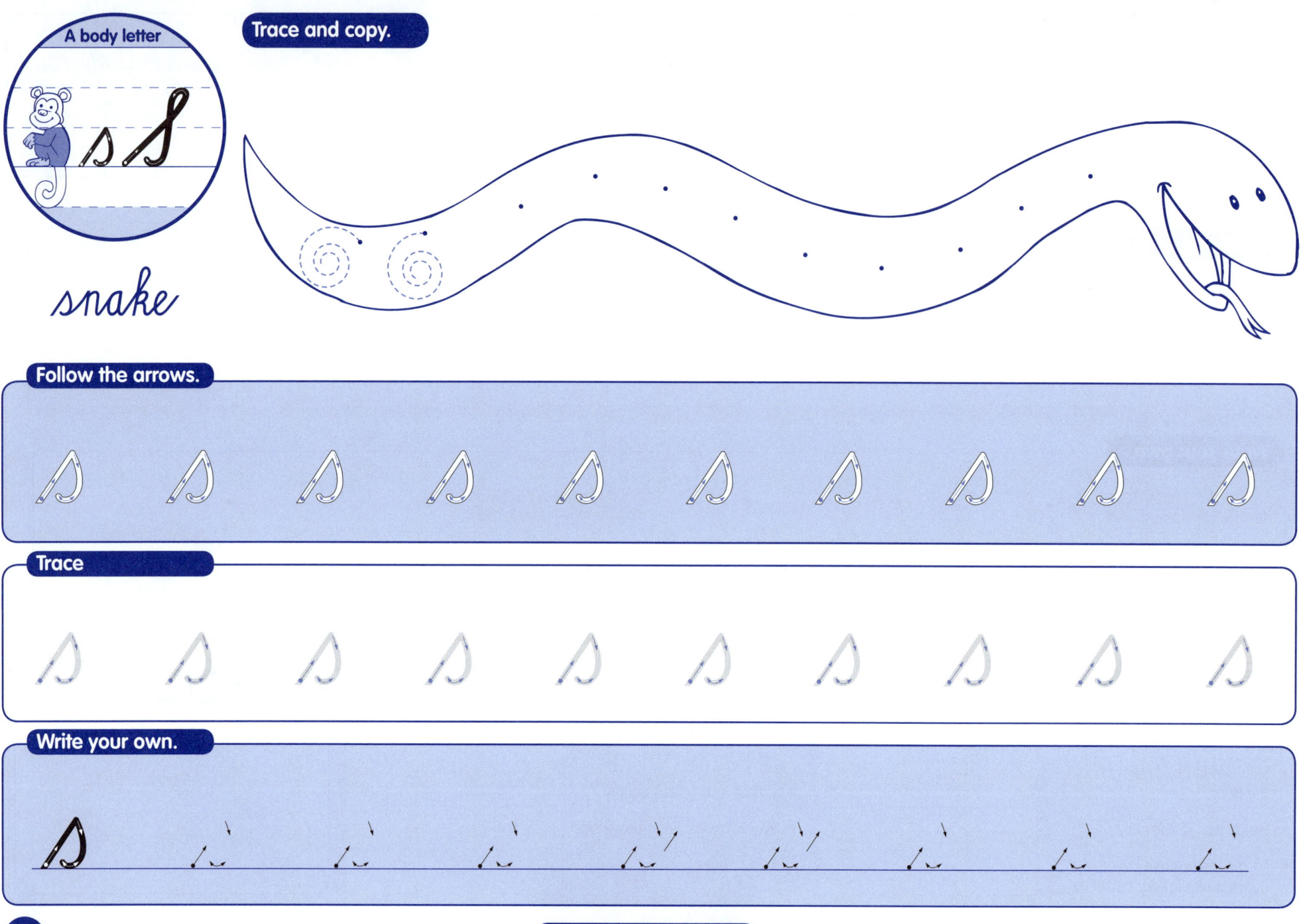

Trace and copy.

snake

Follow the arrows.

Trace

Write your own.

24 Handwriting Today

Prim-Ed Publishing – www.prim-ed.com

Trace

eeee eeee eeee eeee eeee eeee

see   seen   she   so   said   saw

Trace

s s s s s s

Trace

S S S S S S

Write your own.

s

Write your own.

S

Have a go.

Have a go.

Handwriting Today

25

A head and body letter

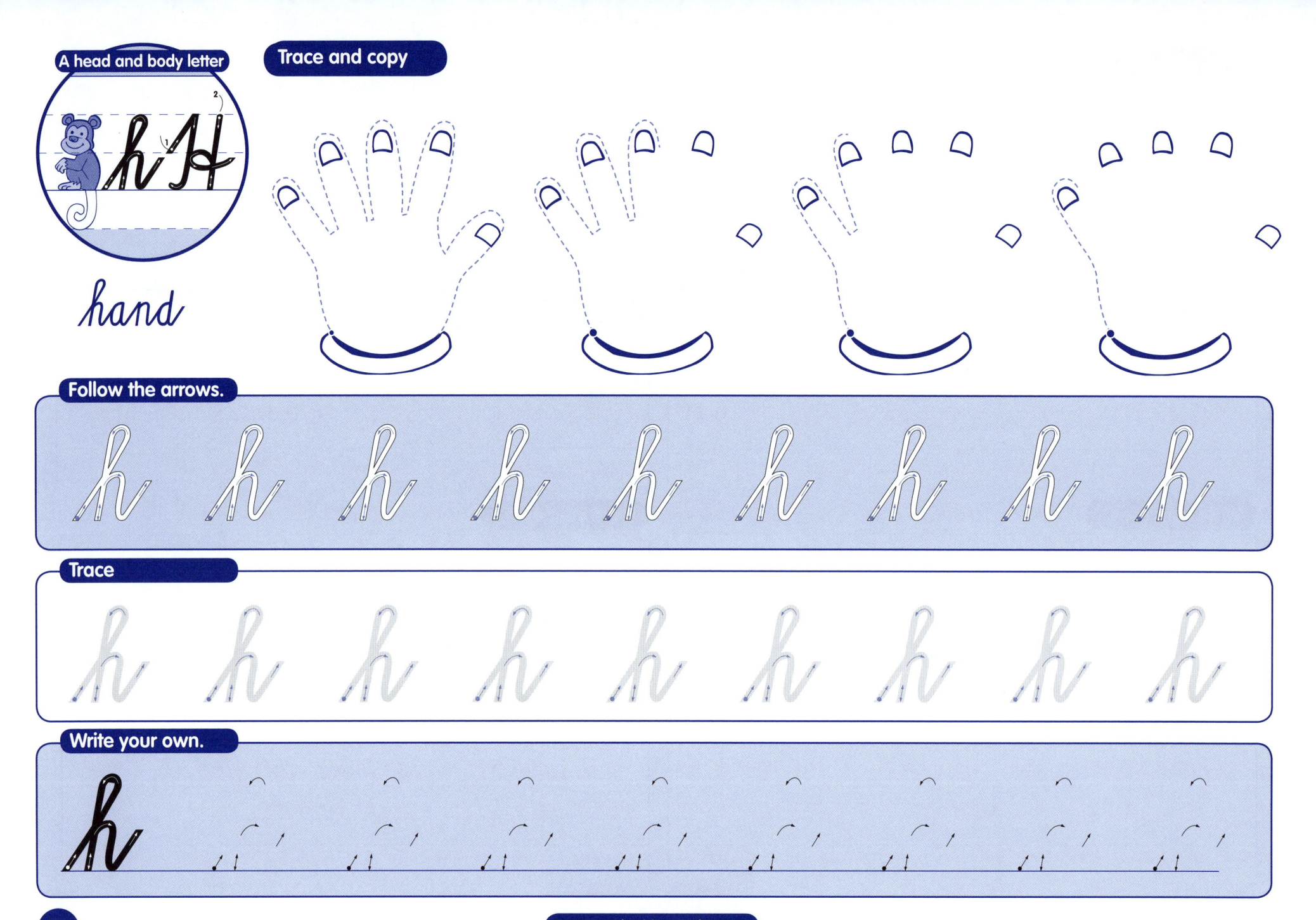

hH

hand

Trace and copy

Follow the arrows.

h h h h h h h h h

Trace

h h h h h h h h h

Write your own.

h

26 Handwriting Today

Prim-Ed Publishing – www.prim-ed.com

Trace

mm mm mm mm mm

he had has her here his

Trace

h h h h h h

Trace

H H H H H H

Write your own.

h

Write your own.

H

Have a go.

Have a go.

Handwriting Today

A head and body letter

Trace and copy

kettle

Follow the arrows.

Trace

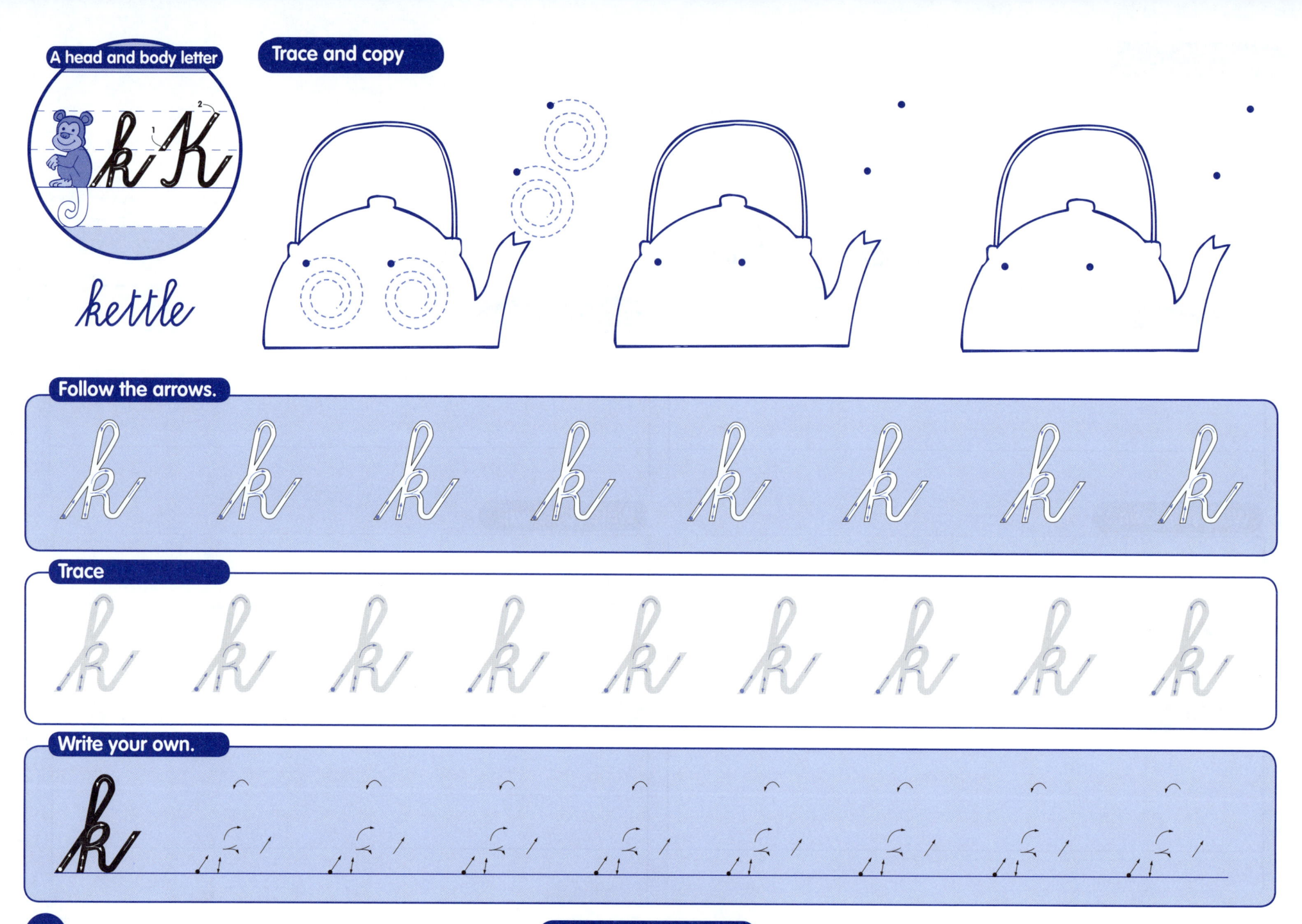

Write your own.

28 — Handwriting Today

Prim-Ed Publishing – www.prim-ed.com

Trace

kitten   kite   knee   kind   key   kid

Trace
k k k k k k

Write your own.
k

Have a go.

Trace
K K K K K K

Write your own.
K

Have a go.

Handwriting Today

29

A body letter

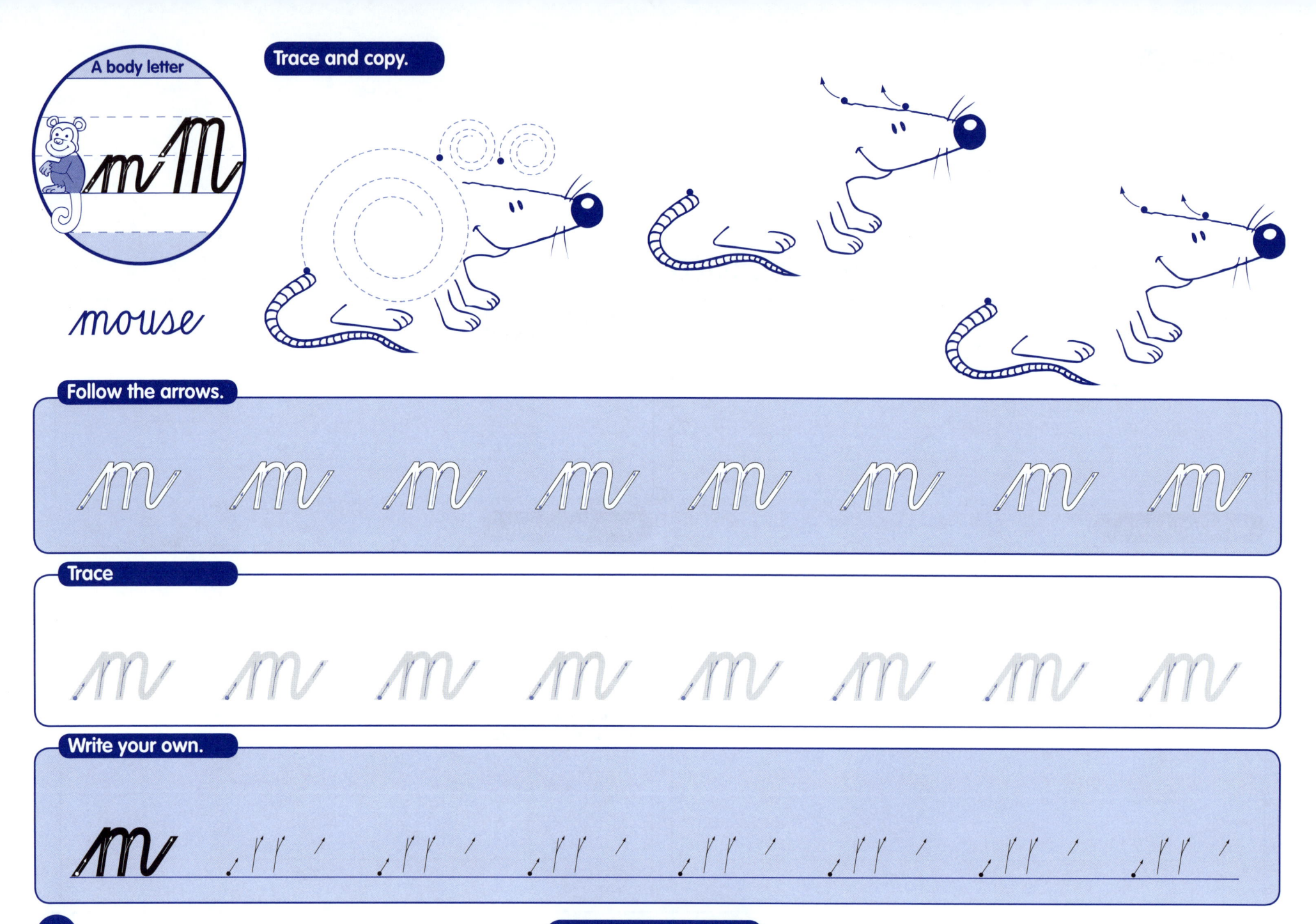

mM

mouse

Trace and copy.

Follow the arrows.

m m m m m m m m

Trace

m m m m m m m m

Write your own.

m

30   Handwriting Today   Prim-Ed Publishing – www.prim-ed.com

Trace

m m m m m

my mum man make may much me

Trace

m m m m m

Trace

M M M M M

Write your own.

m

Write your own.

M

Have a go.

Have a go.

Handwriting Today

31

A body letter

n N

necklace

Trace and copy.

Follow the arrows.

Trace

Write your own.

32

Handwriting Today

Prim-Ed Publishing – www.prim-ed.com

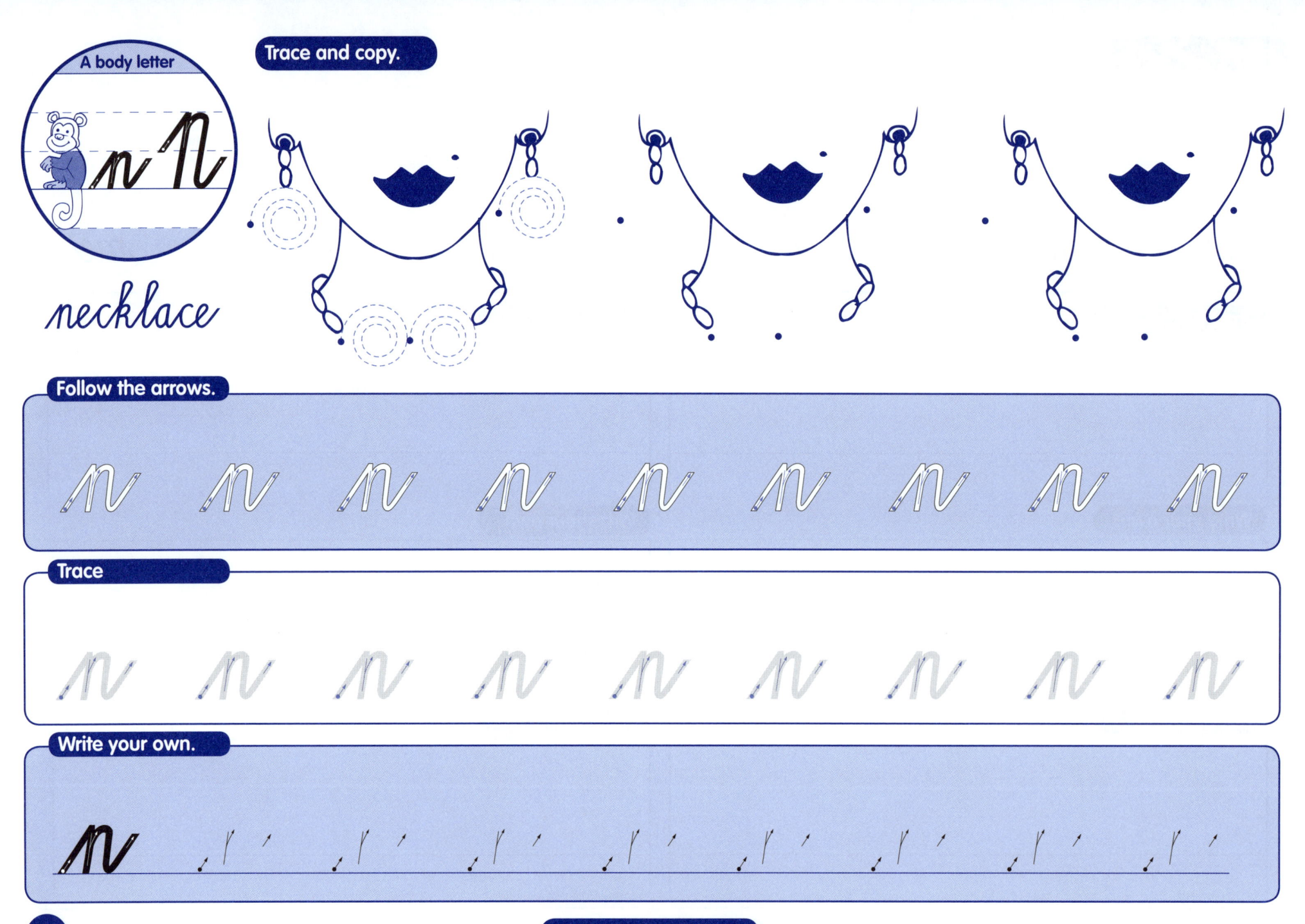

Trace

no   name   new   not   now   night

Trace

Trace

Write your own.

Write your own.

Have a go.

Have a go.

Handwriting Today

33

A body and tail letter

p P

peacock

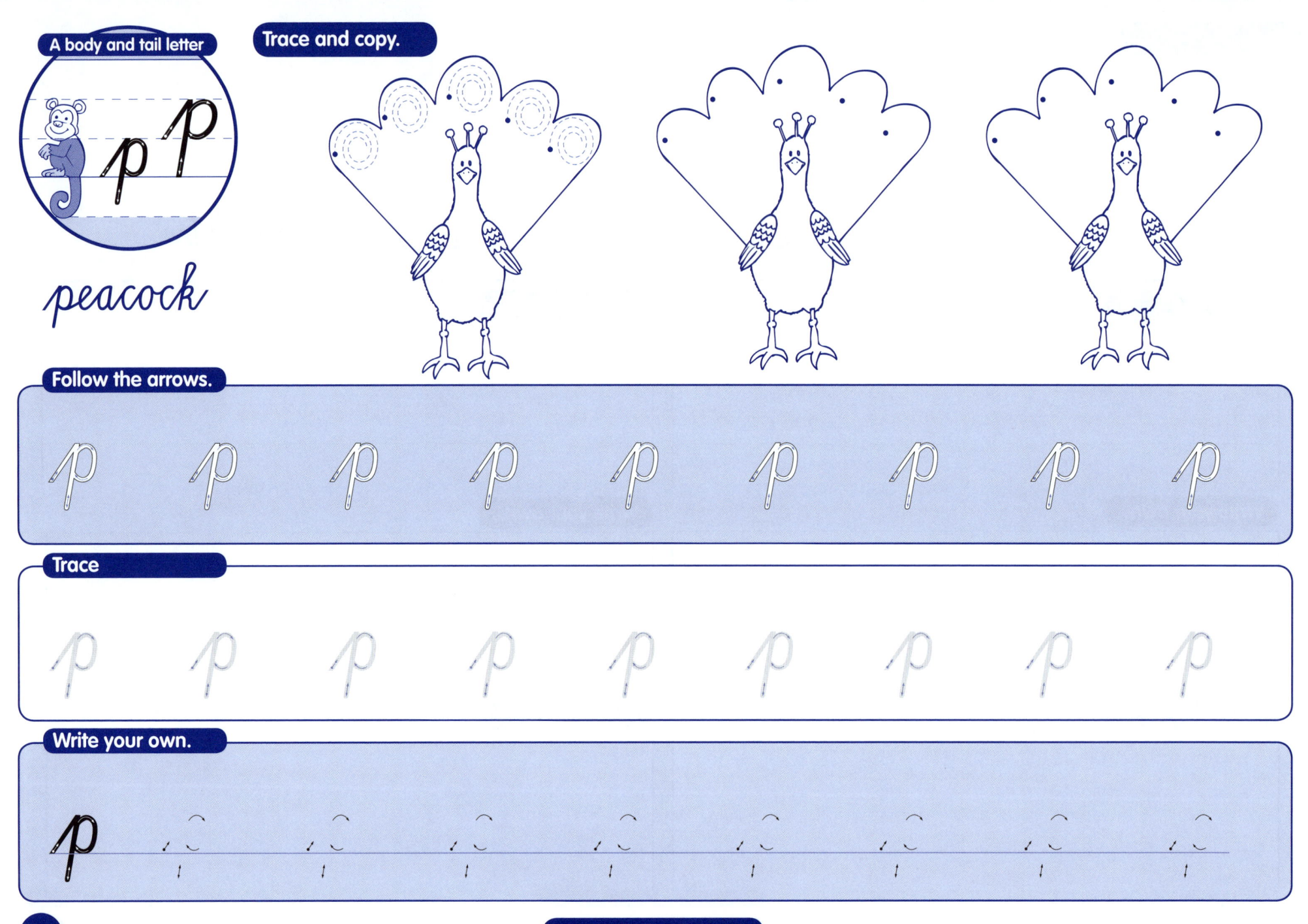

Trace and copy.

Follow the arrows.

Trace

Write your own.

34

Handwriting Today

Prim-Ed Publishing – www.prim-ed.com

Trace

play   pull   put   push   people   pear

Trace

Write your own.

p

Have a go.

Trace

Write your own.

p

Have a go.

Handwriting Today

A body letter

Trace and copy.

rabbit

Follow the arrows.

Trace

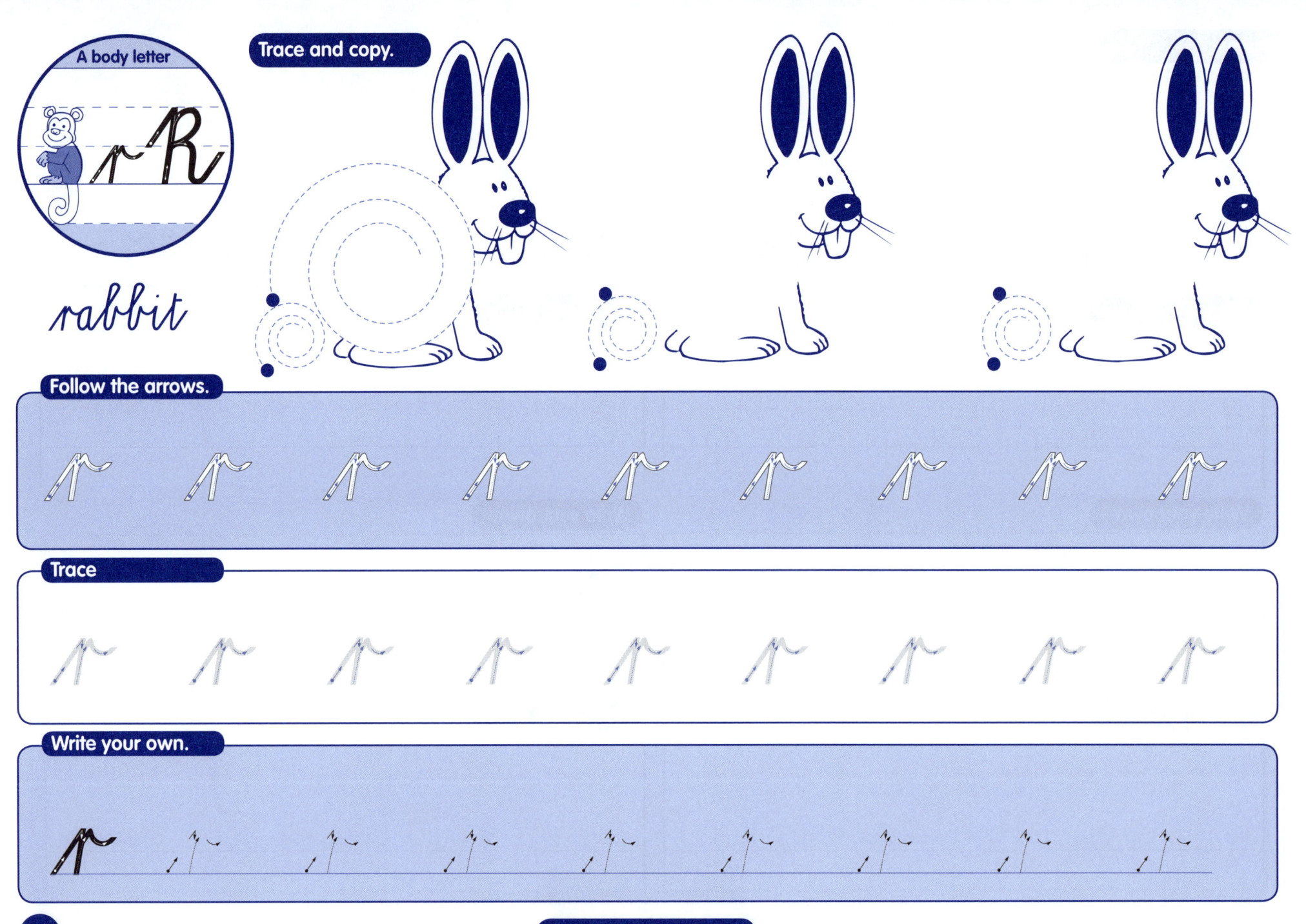

Write your own.

36 — Handwriting Today — Prim-Ed Publishing – www.prim-ed.com

Trace

rrrrrrr

ran   rain   run   race   read   red

Trace

r r r r r r r

Trace

R R R R R R

Write your own.

r

Write your own.

R

Have a go.

Have a go.

A body letter

Trace and copy.

xylophone

Follow the arrows.

Trace

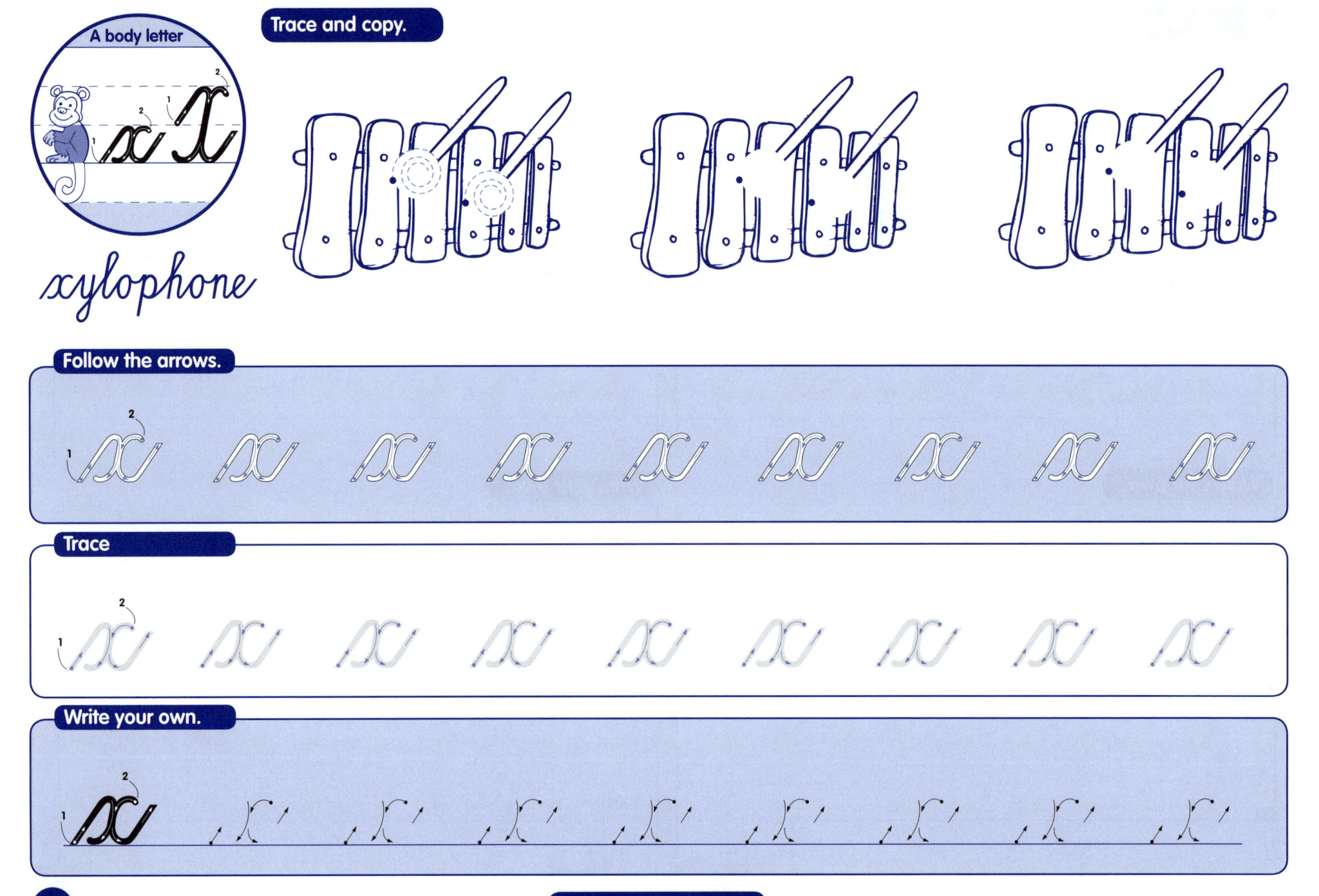

Write your own.

38 — Handwriting Today

Prim-Ed Publishing – www.prim-ed.com

Trace

x-ray   tax   fox   six   ox   wax

Trace

x x x x x x

X X X X X X

Write your own.

x

X

Have a go.

Handwriting Today

A body and tail letter

Trace and copy.

zigzag

Follow the arrows.

Trace

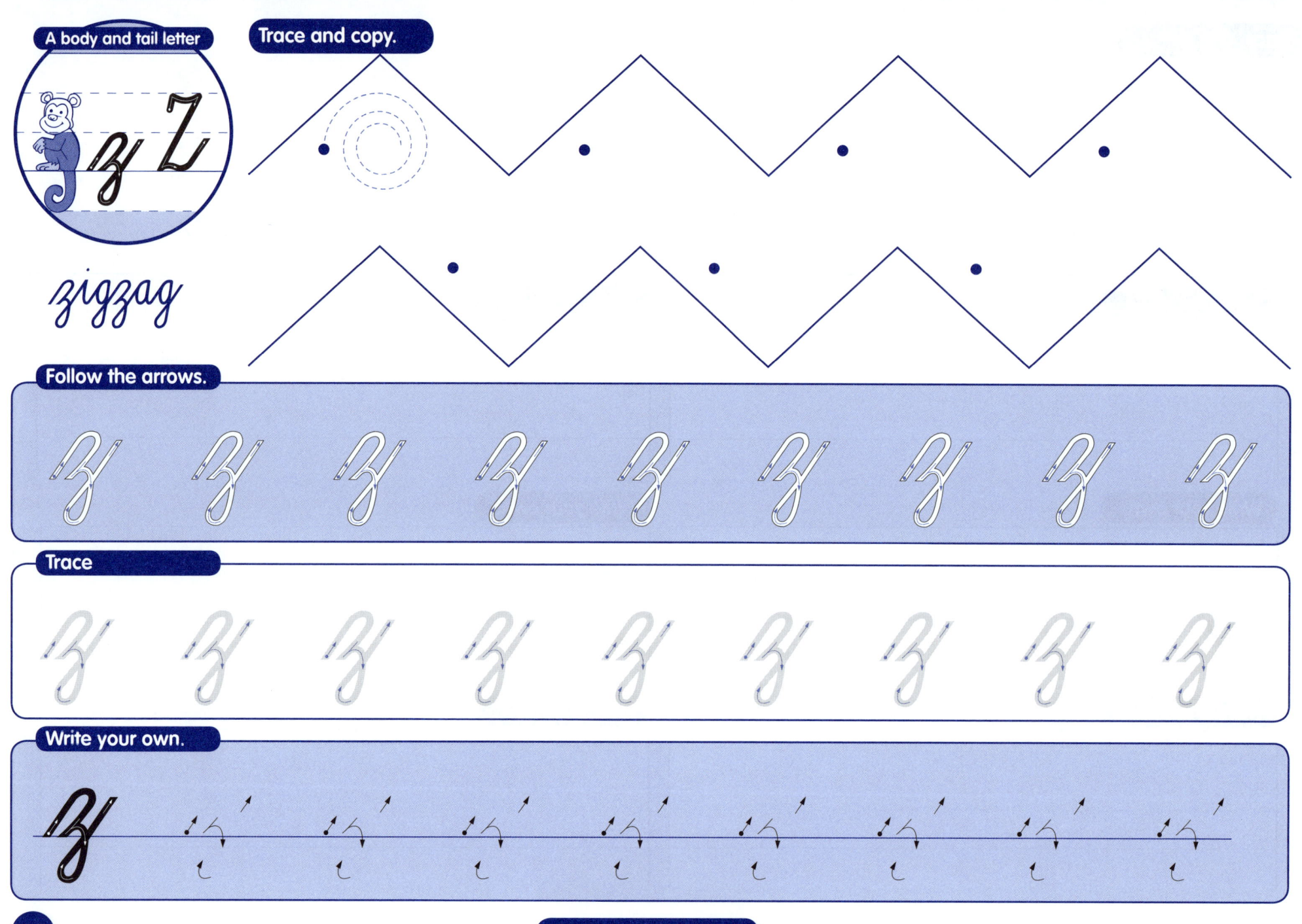

Write your own.

40

Handwriting Today

Prim-Ed Publishing – www.prim-ed.com

Trace

zoo zone zigzag zero zinc zoom

Trace

Write your own.

Have a go.

Trace

Write your own.

Have a go.

Handwriting Today

41

Review: s h k m n p r x z

Trace

Trace and copy.

s h k m n r p x z

Write your own.

42 Handwriting Today

Prim-Ed Publishing – www.prim-ed.com

S H K M N P R X Z

Trace and copy.

S H K M N P R X Z

Write your own.

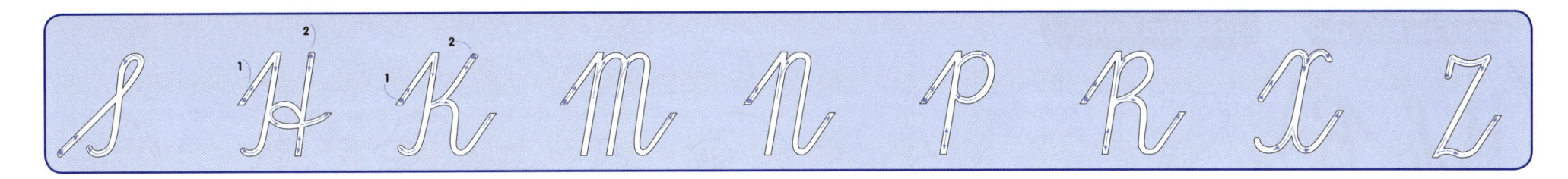

Assessment

- Uses a sharp pencil.
- Sits tall with both feet on the floor.
- Holds pencil correctly.
- Forms lower case downstroke letters correctly.

	Demonstrated	Needs further opportunity

- Forms upper case letters correctly.
- Writes neatly and legibly.
- Writes on the lines provided.

	Demonstrated	Needs further opportunity

General Comment

Handwriting Today

A head and body letter

b B

bird

Trace and copy.

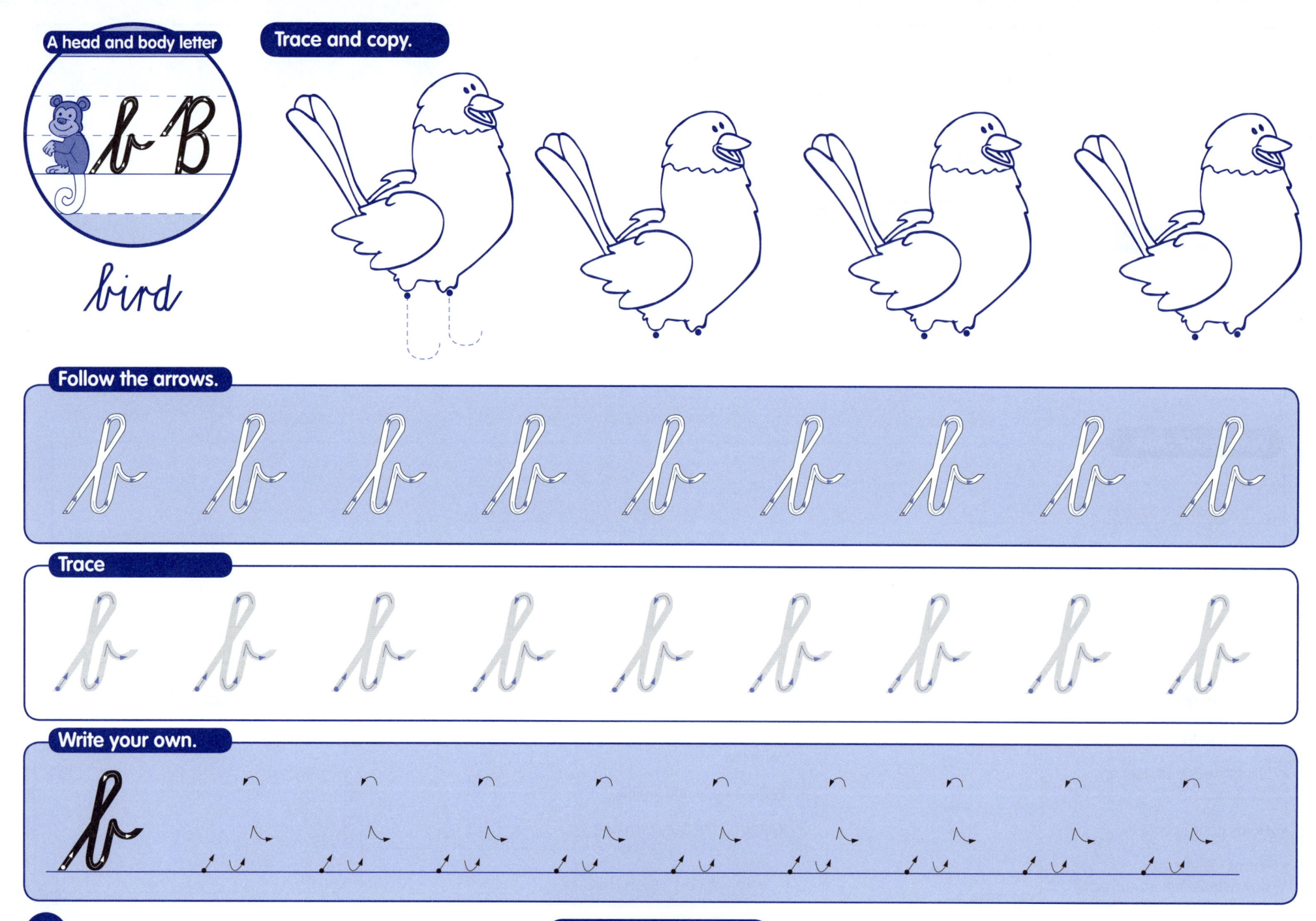

Follow the arrows.

Trace

Write your own.

44

Handwriting Today

Prim-Ed Publishing – www.prim-ed.com

Trace

big   back   ball   be   because   boy

Trace

b b b b b b

Write your own.

b

Have a go.

Trace

B B B B B B

Write your own.

B

Have a go.

Handwriting Today

45

Prim-Ed Publishing – www.prim-ed.com

A body letter

ice-cream

Trace and copy.

Follow the arrows.

Trace

Write your own.

46

Handwriting Today

Prim-Ed Publishing – www.prim-ed.com

Trace

I is in it if ice

Trace

i i i i i i i

Write your own.

i

Have a go.

Trace

I I I I I I I

Write your own.

I

Have a go.

A body and tail letter

j J

jeans

Trace and copy.

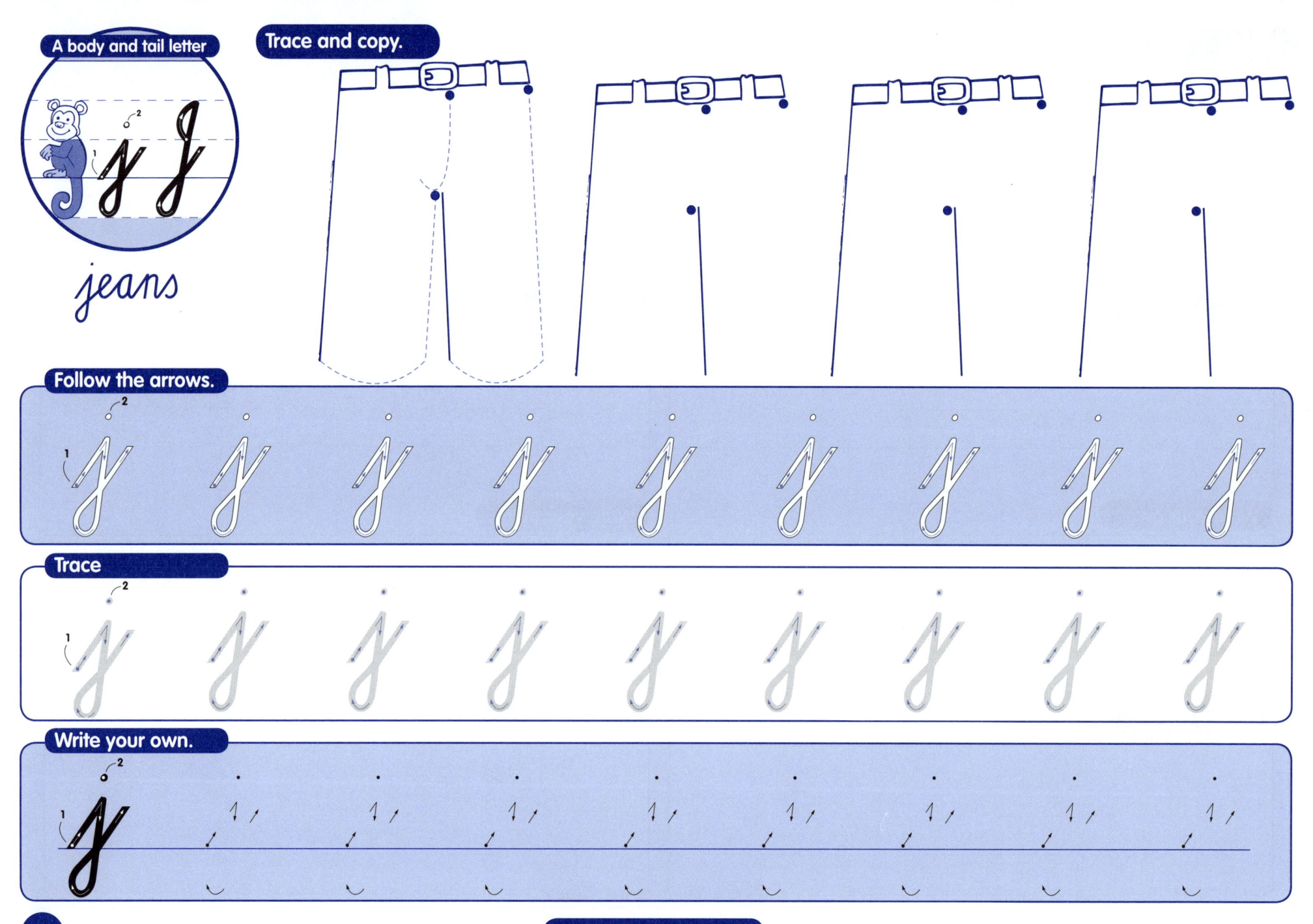

Follow the arrows.

Trace

Write your own.

48 Handwriting Today

Prim-Ed Publishing – www.prim-ed.com

Trace

J J J J J J J J J J J J

jug   just   June   July   joke   jog

Trace

j j j j j j

Trace

J J J J J J

Write your own.

j

Write your own.

J

Have a go.

Have a go.

Handwriting Today

49

A head and body letter

ℓ L

ladder

Trace and copy.

Follow the arrows.

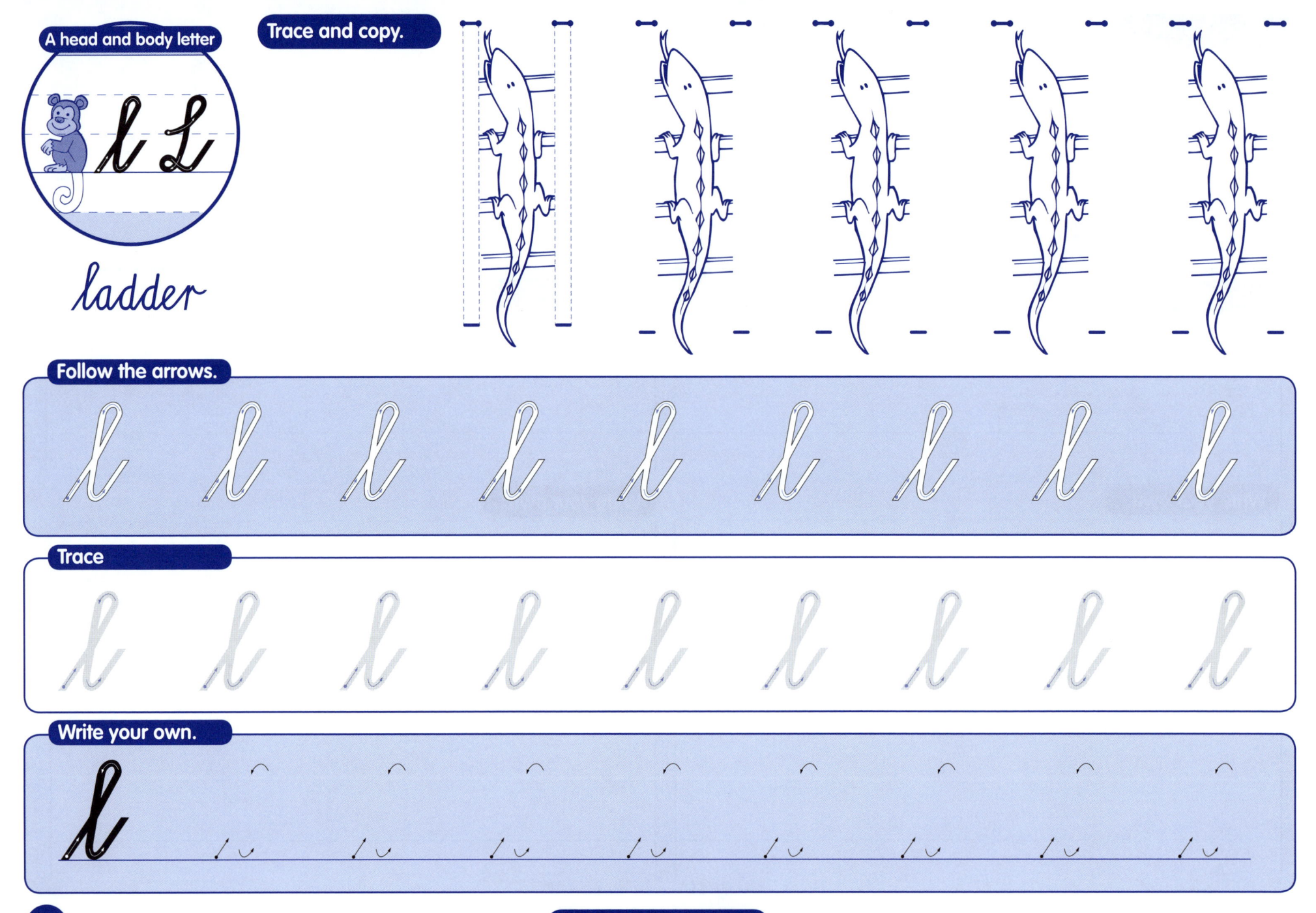

Trace

Write your own.

50 — Handwriting Today — Prim-Ed Publishing – www.prim-ed.com

Trace

look   like   last   live   love

Trace

l l l l l l

Trace

L L L L L L

Write your own.

l

Write your own.

L

Have a go.

Have a go.

A head and body letter

towel

Trace and copy.

Follow the arrows.

Trace

Write your own.

52 — Handwriting Today — Prim-Ed Publishing – www.prim-ed.com

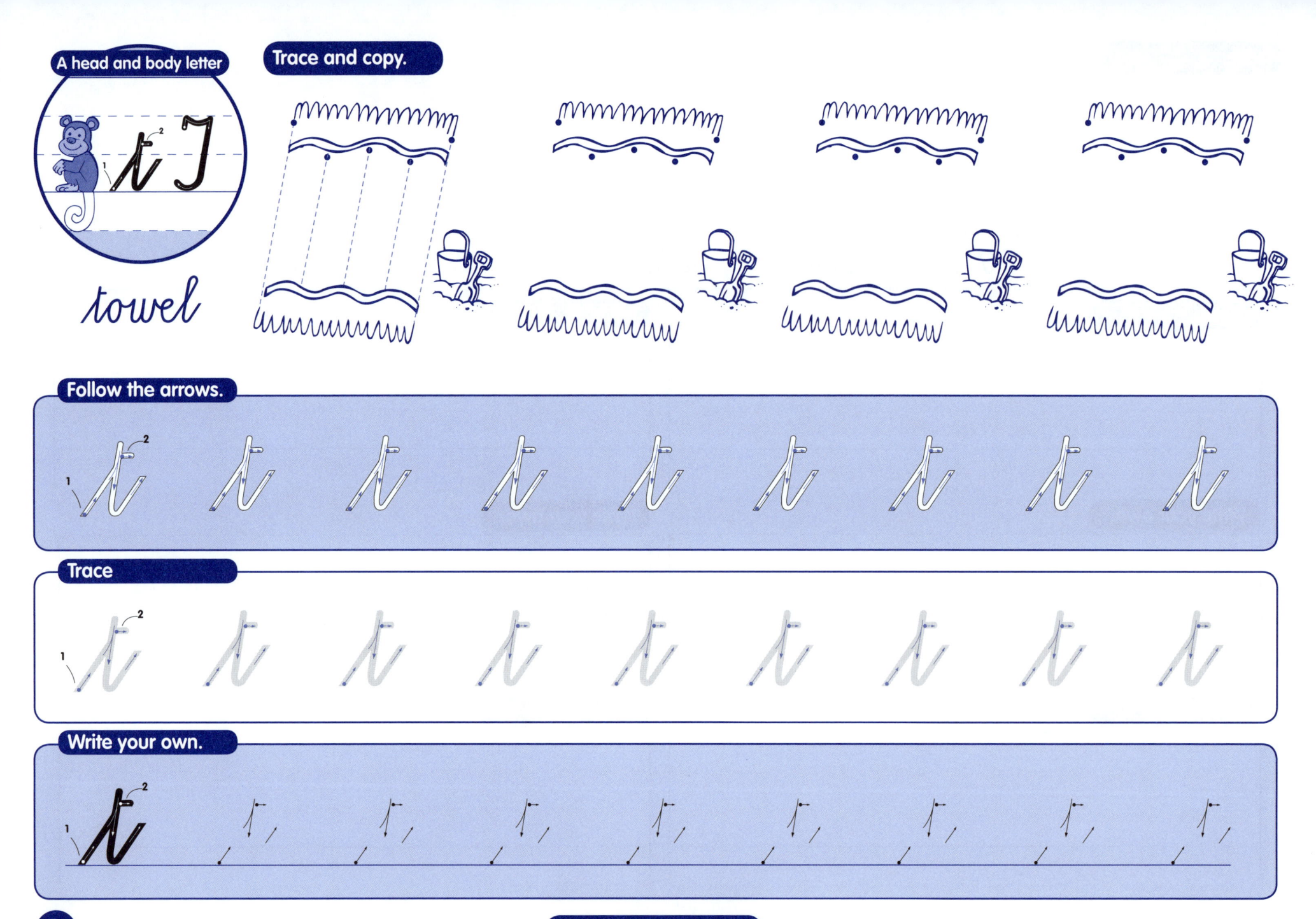

Trace

they this to the that their then there

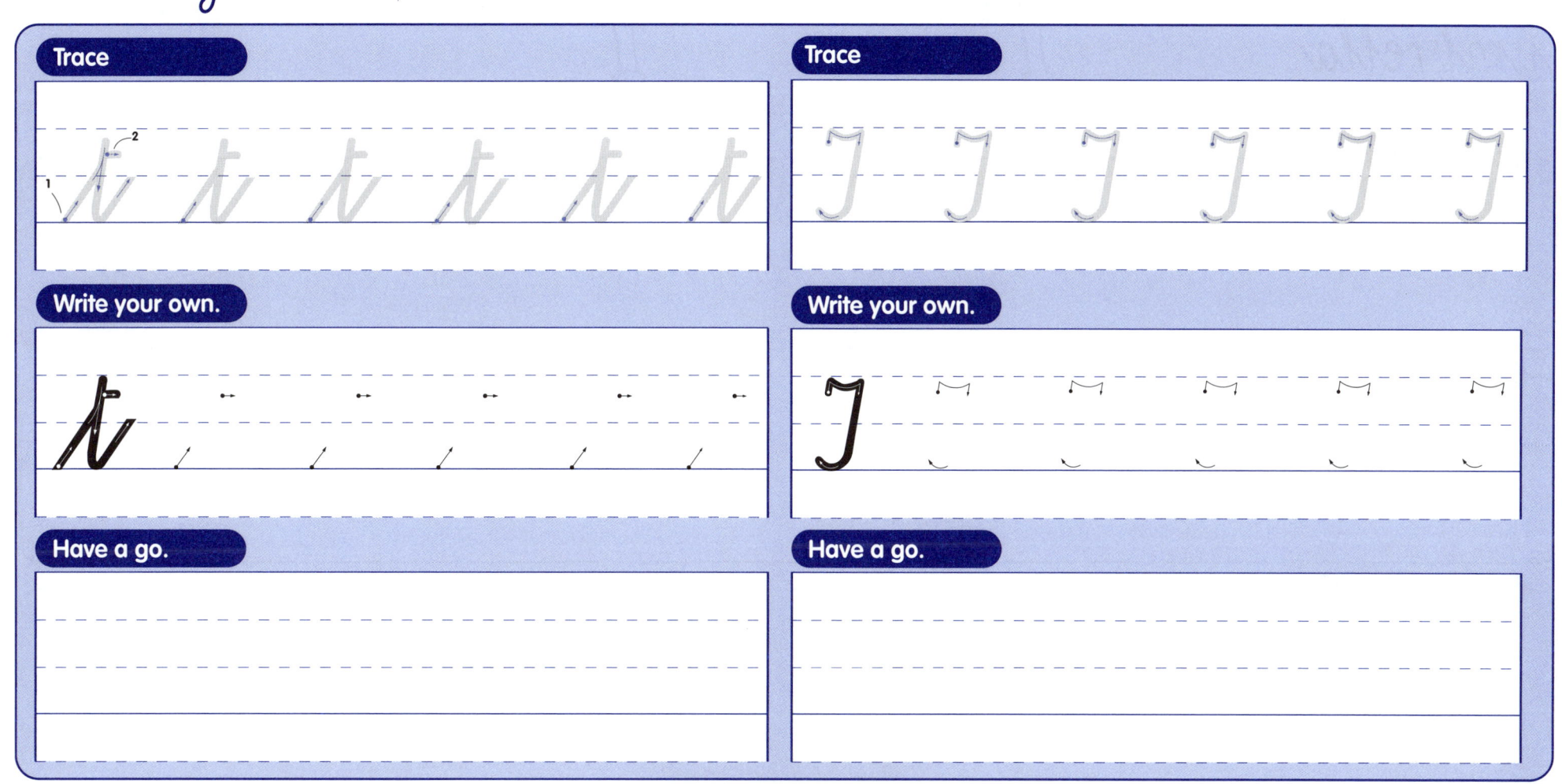

Trace

t t t t t t t

Trace

J J J J J J J

Write your own.

t

Write your own.

J

Have a go.

Have a go.

Handwriting Today

A body letter

umbrella

Trace and copy.

Follow the arrows.

Trace

Write your own.

54

Handwriting Today

Prim-Ed Publishing – www.prim-ed.com

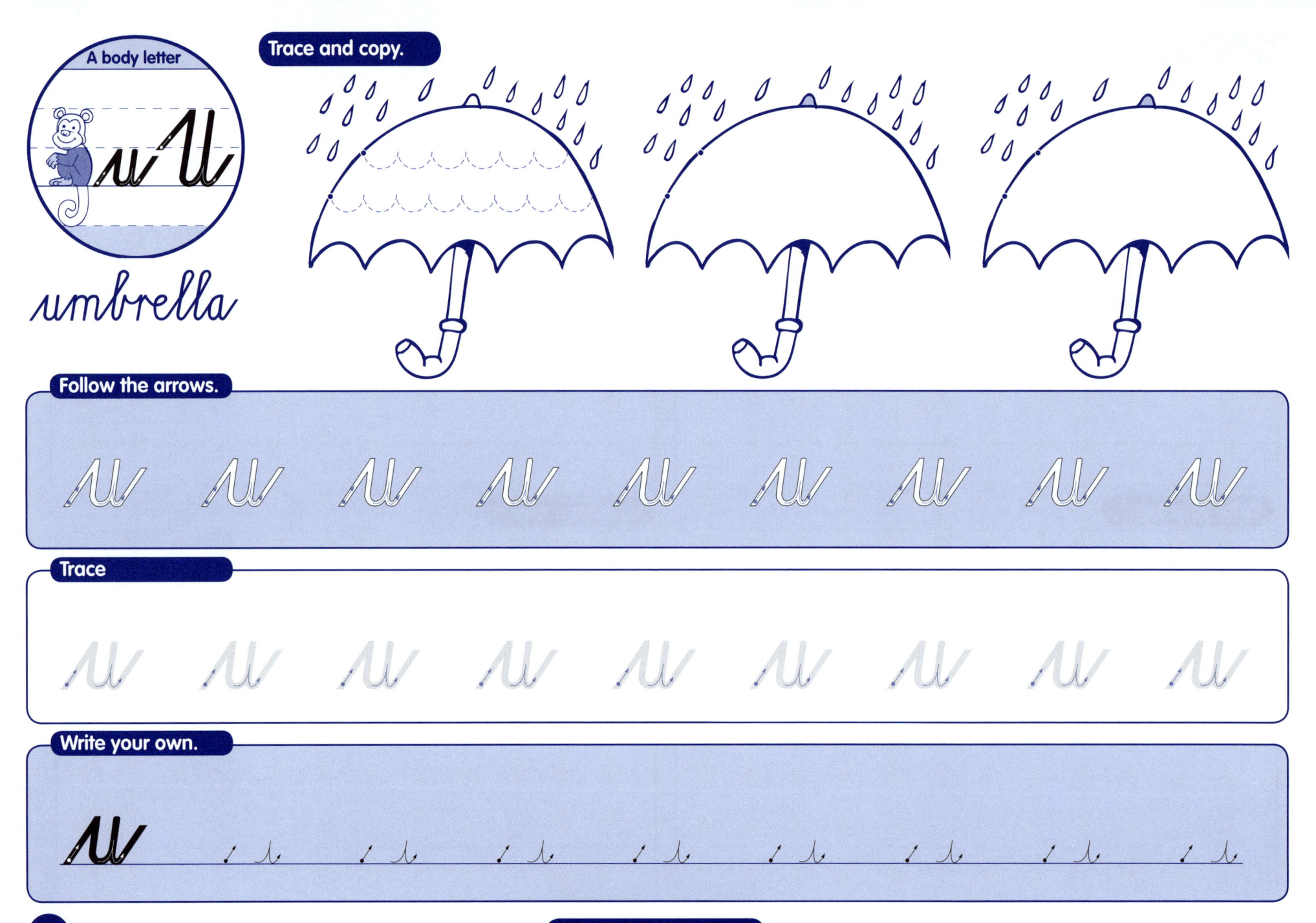

Trace

u u u u u u u u u u u u u u u u u u

undo   us   use   under   uncle   ugly

Trace

Write your own.

u

Have a go.

Trace

Write your own.

Have a go.

Handwriting Today

55

A body letter

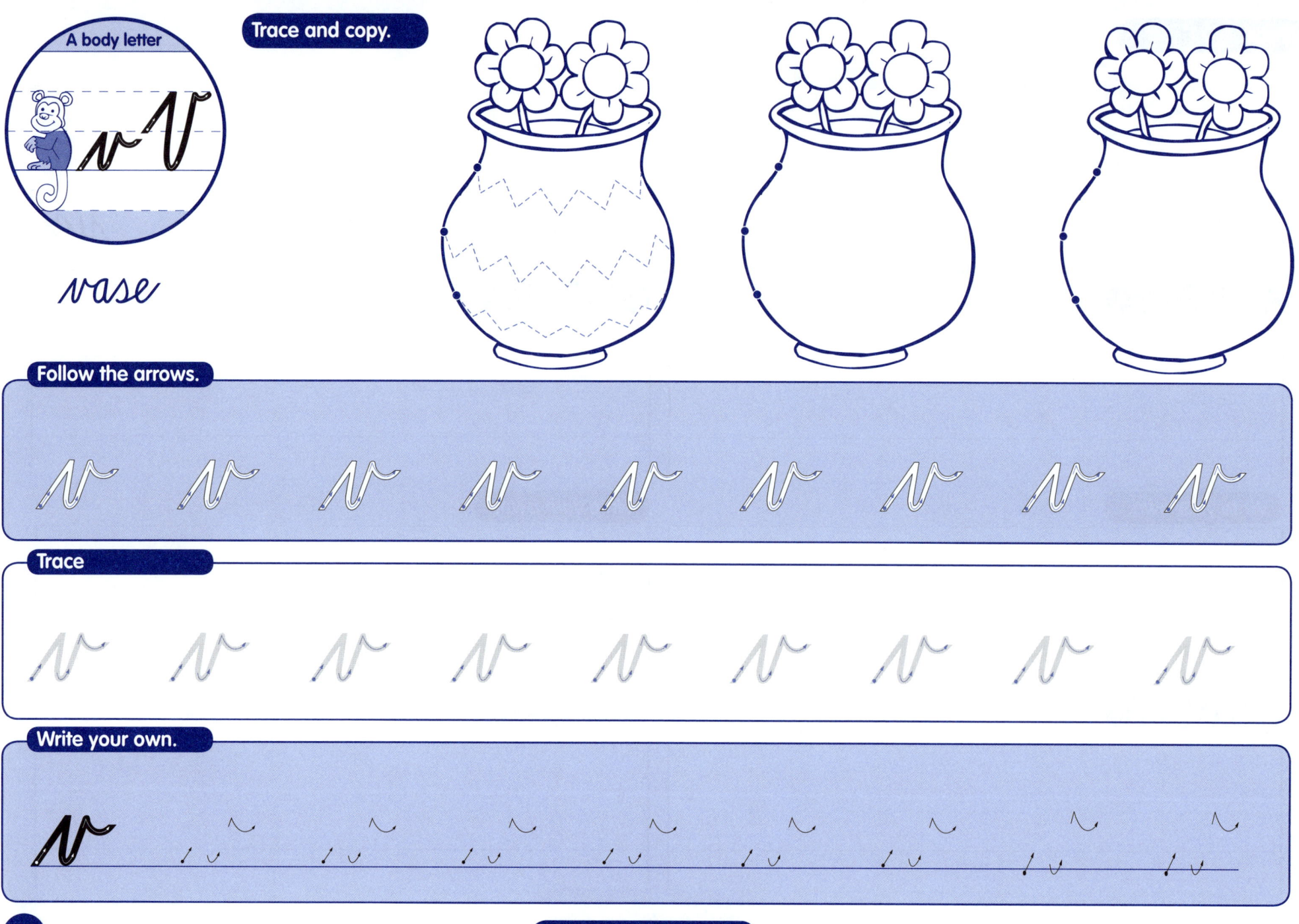

Trace and copy.

vase

Follow the arrows.

Trace

Write your own.

56 — Handwriting Today

Prim-Ed Publishing – www.prim-ed.com

Trace

very   van   video   visit   view   vote

Trace

Trace

Write your own.

Write your own.

Have a go.

Have a go.

Handwriting Today

Prim-Ed Publishing – www.prim-ed.com

A body letter

Trace and copy.

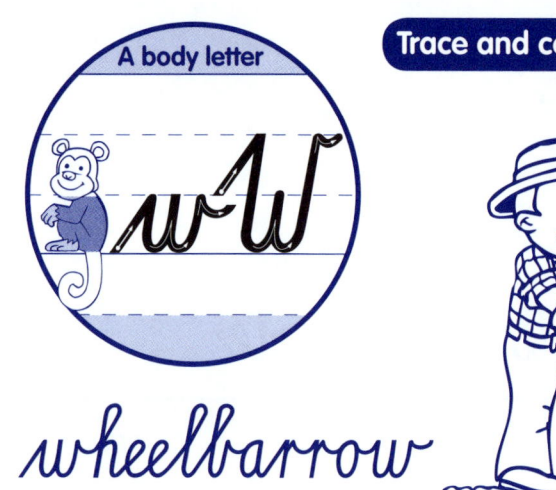

w W

wheelbarrow

Follow the arrows.

Trace

Write your own.

58

Handwriting Today

Prim-Ed Publishing – www.prim-ed.com

Trace

we went was want were with would

Trace

Trace

Write your own.

w

Write your own.

W

Have a go.

Have a go.

Handwriting Today

59

Prim-Ed Publishing – www.prim-ed.com

A body and tail letter

y Y

yacht

Trace and copy

Follow the arrows.

y y y y y y y y y

Trace

y y y y y y y y y

Write your own.

y

60

Handwriting Today

Prim-Ed Publishing – www.prim-ed.com

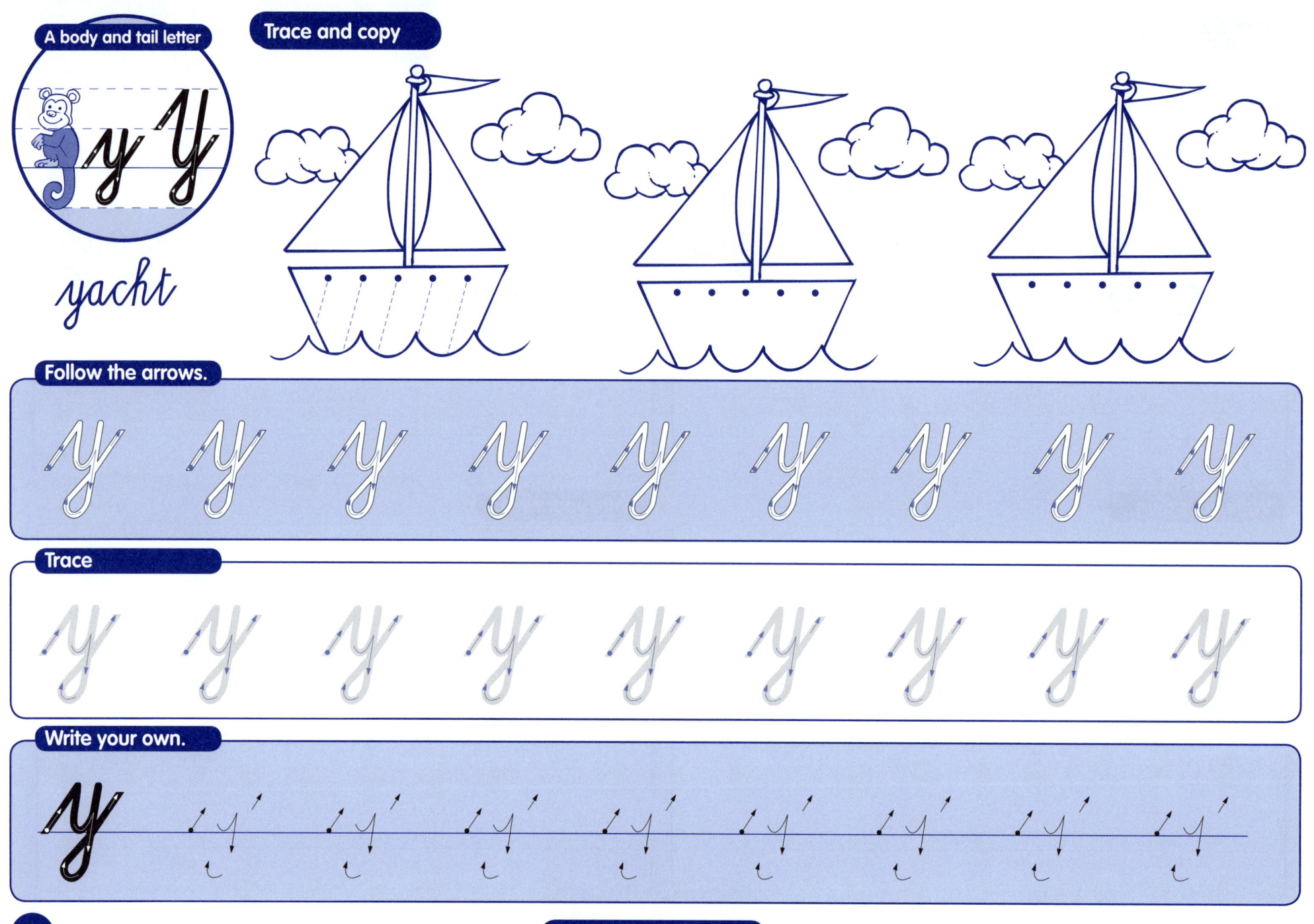

Trace

you   yes   your   year   yellow   yummy

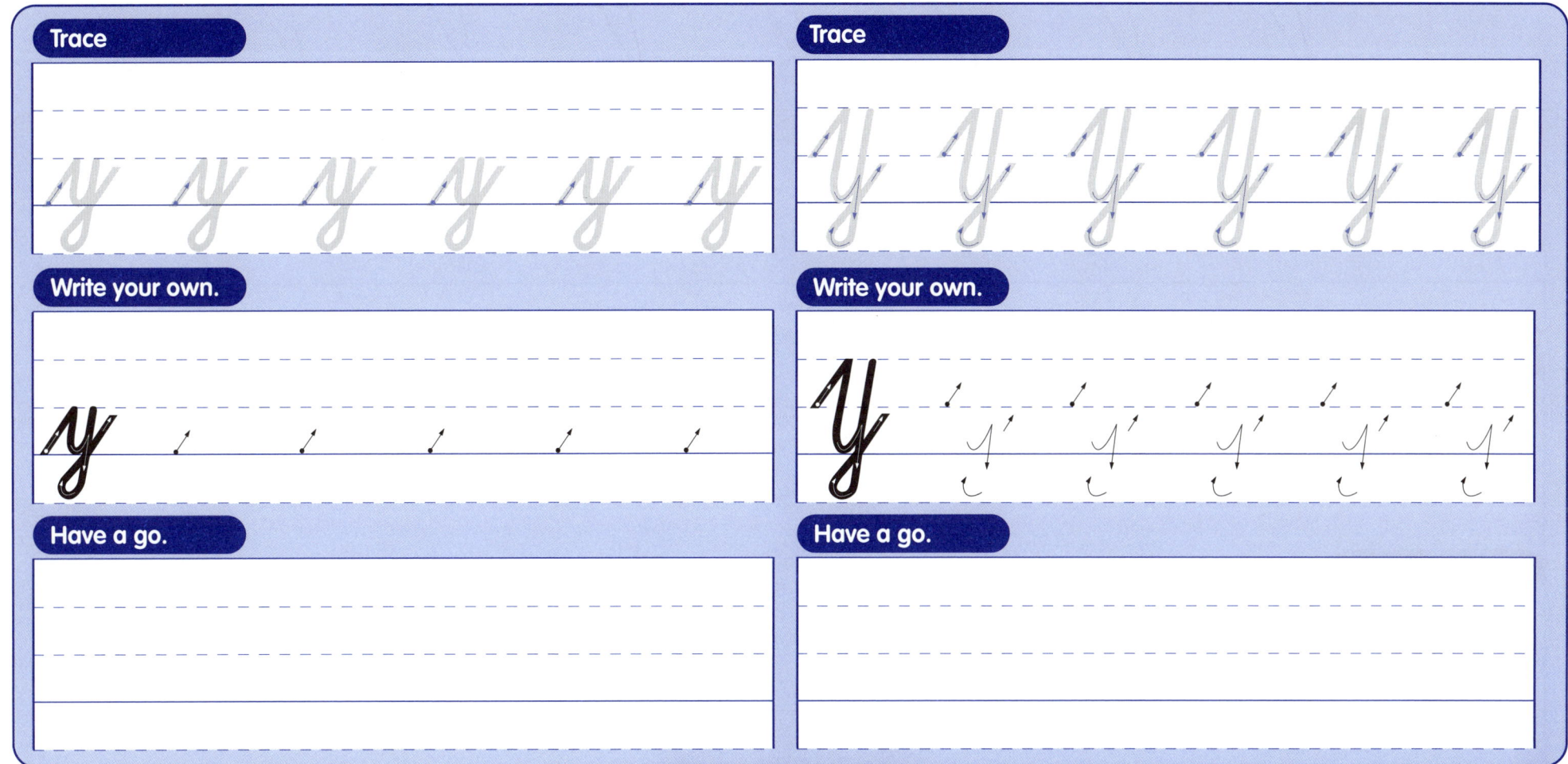

Trace

Trace

Write your own.

Write your own.

Have a go.

Have a go.

Handwriting Today

61

Review: b j l t u v w y

Trace

Trace and copy.

b j l t u v w y

Write your own.

Have a go.

62

Handwriting Today

Prim-Ed Publishing – www.prim-ed.com

B J L T U V W Y

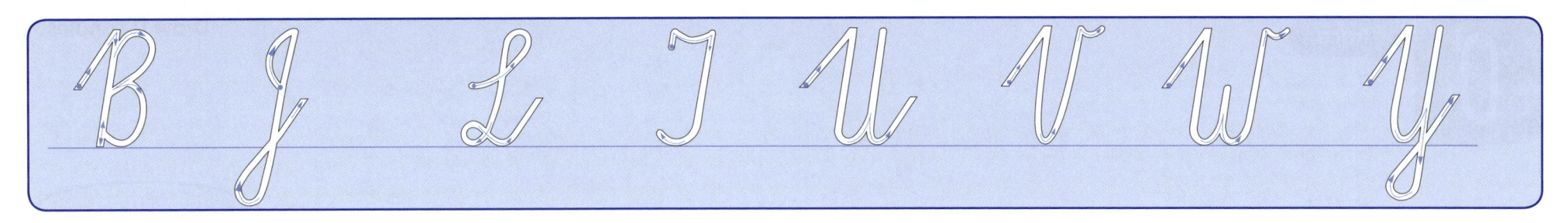

Trace and copy.

B J L T U V W Y

Write your own.

Assessment

	Demonstrated	Needs further opportunity
Uses a sharp pencil.		
Sits tall with both feet on the floor.		
Holds pencil correctly.		
Forms lower case downstroke letters correctly.		

	Demonstrated	Needs further opportunity
Forms upper case letters correctly.		
Writes neatly and legibly.		
Writes on the lines provided.		

General Comment

0

Trace

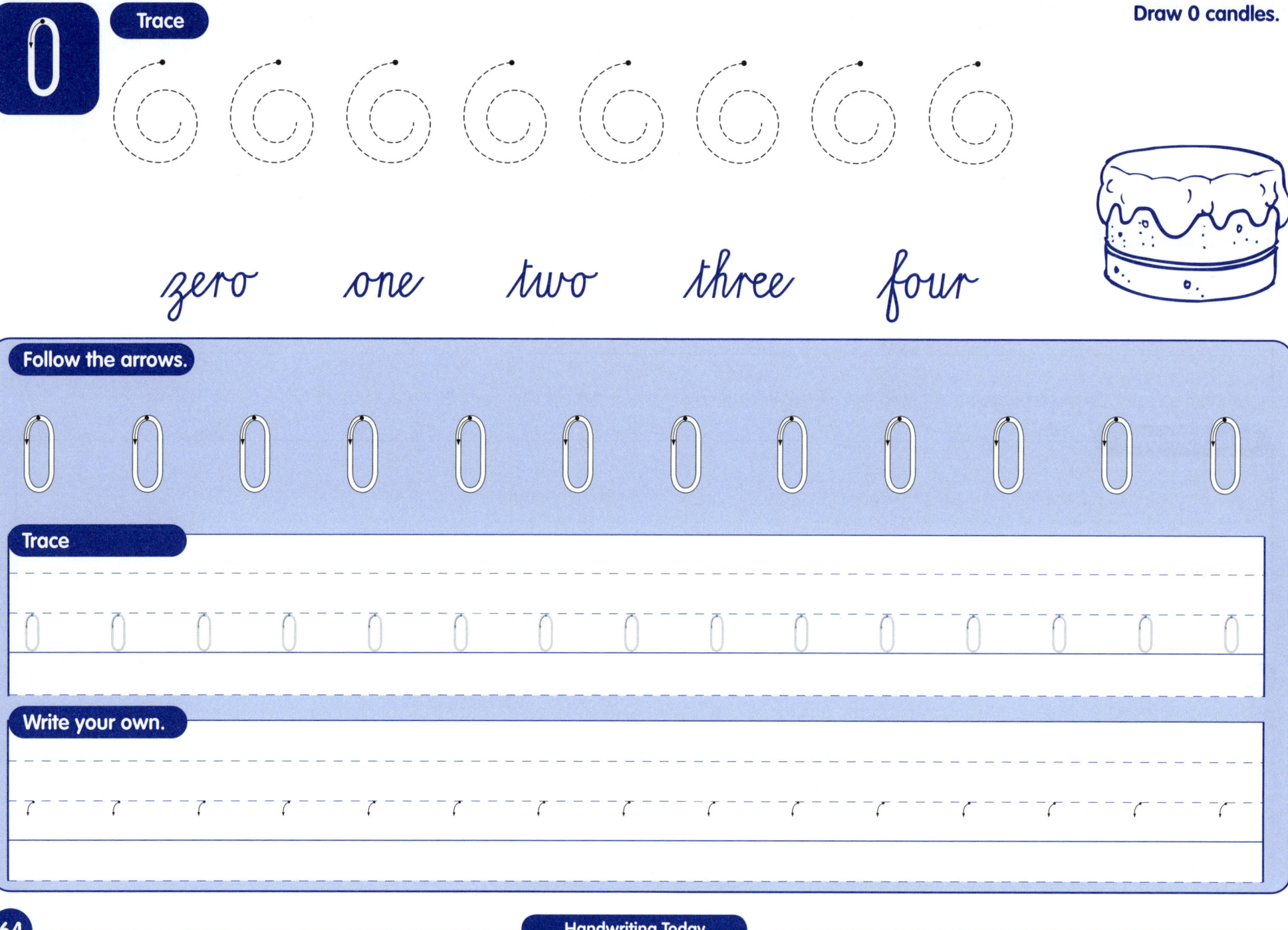

Draw 0 candles.

zero   one   two   three   four

Follow the arrows.

Trace

Write your own.

64 — Handwriting Today

Prim-Ed Publishing – www.prim-ed.com

Trace

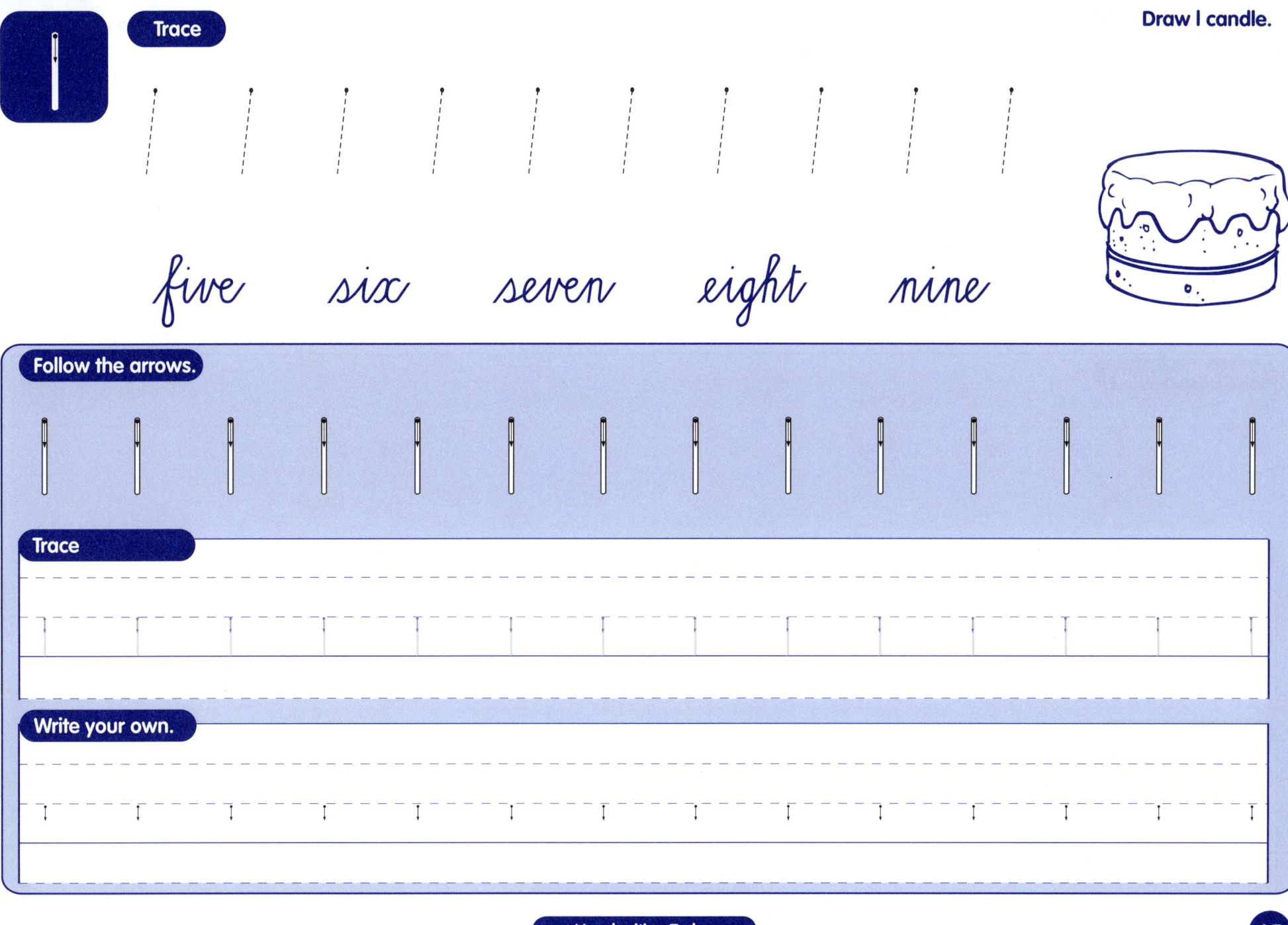

Draw 1 candle.

five   six   seven   eight   nine

Follow the arrows.

Trace

Write your own.

Handwriting Today

65

2 Trace

Draw 2 candles.

zero   one   two   three   four

Follow the arrows.

2 2 2 2 2 2 2 2 2 2 2

Trace

Write your own.

66 Handwriting Today

Prim-Ed Publishing – www.prim-ed.com

3

Trace

Draw 3 candles.

five   six   seven   eight   nine

Follow the arrows.

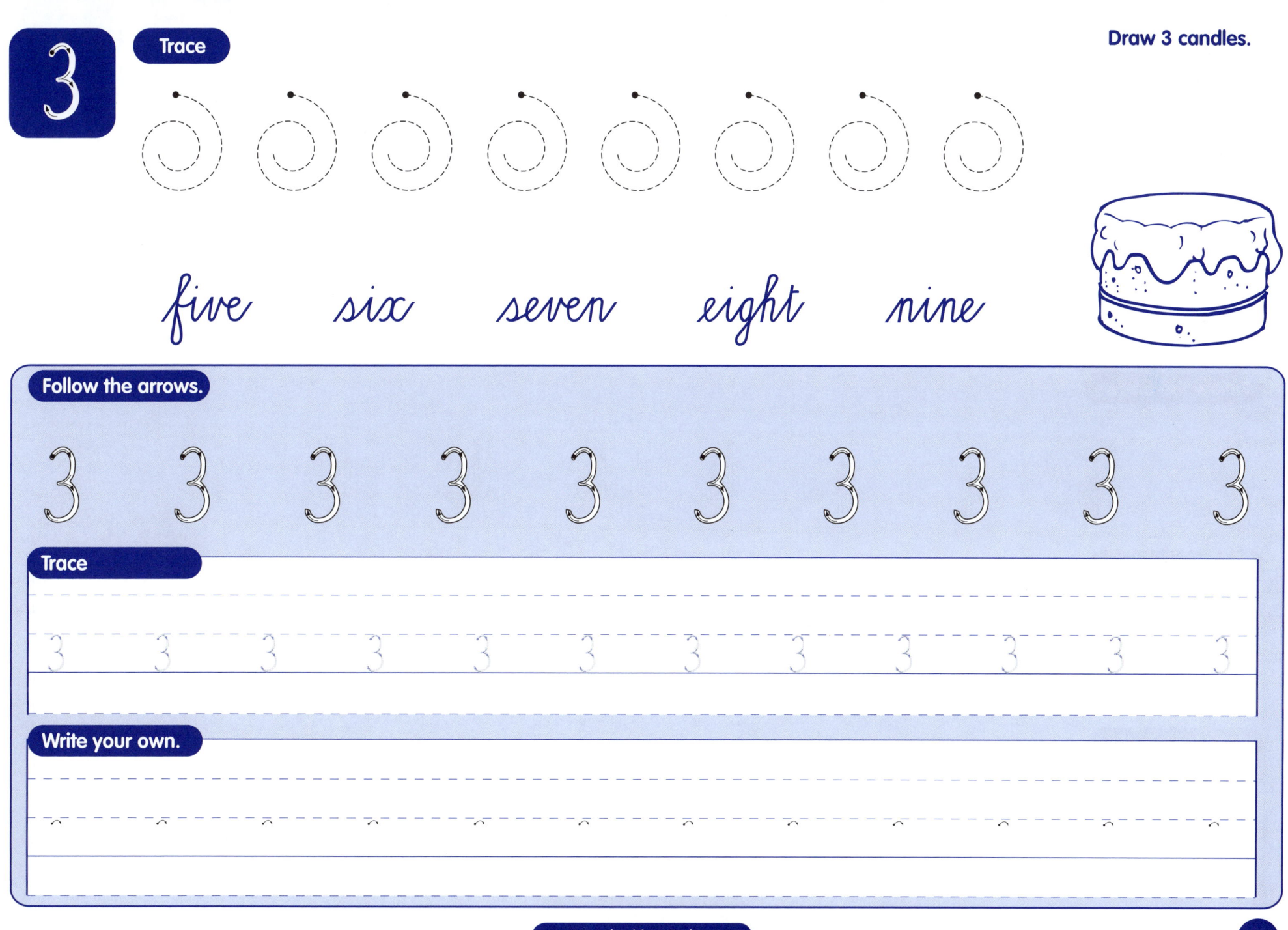

3 3 3 3 3 3 3 3 3 3

Trace

3 3 3 3 3 3 3 3 3 3 3 3

Write your own.

Trace

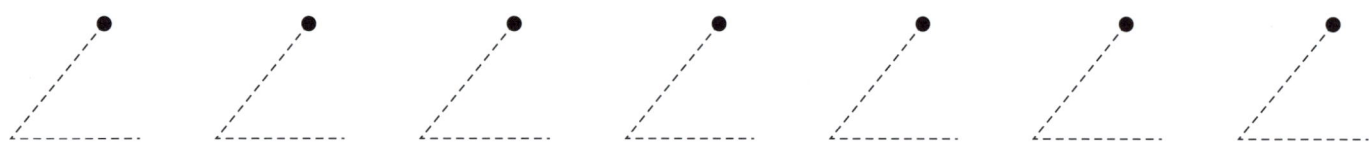

Draw 4 candles.

zero one two three four

Follow the arrows.

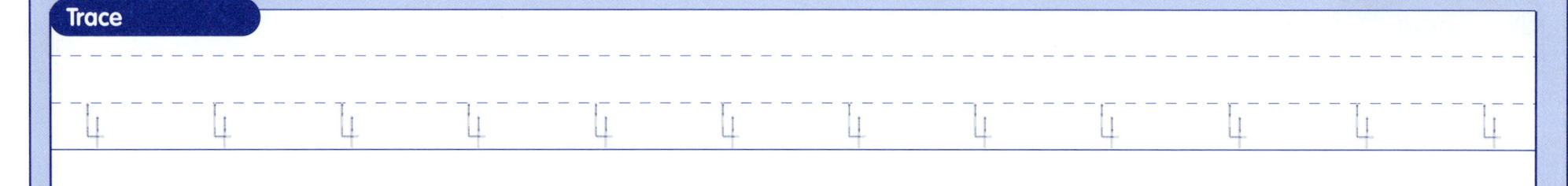

4 4 4 4 4 4 4 4 4 4

Trace

Write your own.

68   Handwriting Today

5 Trace

Draw 5 candles.

five   six   seven   eight   nine

Follow the arrows.

5 5 5 5 5 5 5 5 5 5 5

Trace

5 5 5 5 5 5 5 5 5 5 5 5

Write your own.

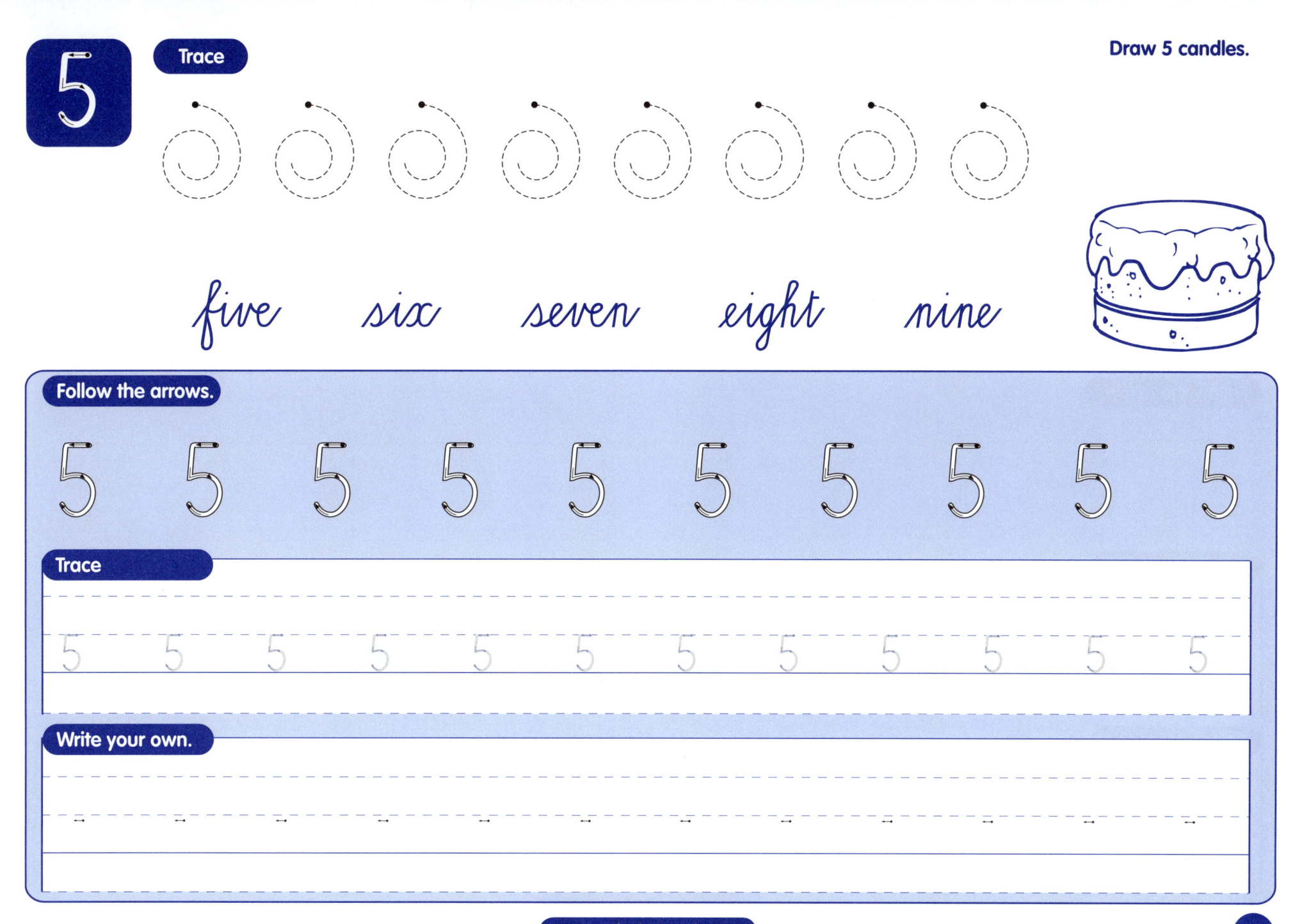

Handwriting Today

Prim-Ed Publishing – www.prim-ed.com

69

6

Trace

Draw 6 candles.

zero   one   two   three   four

Follow the arrows.

Trace

Write your own.

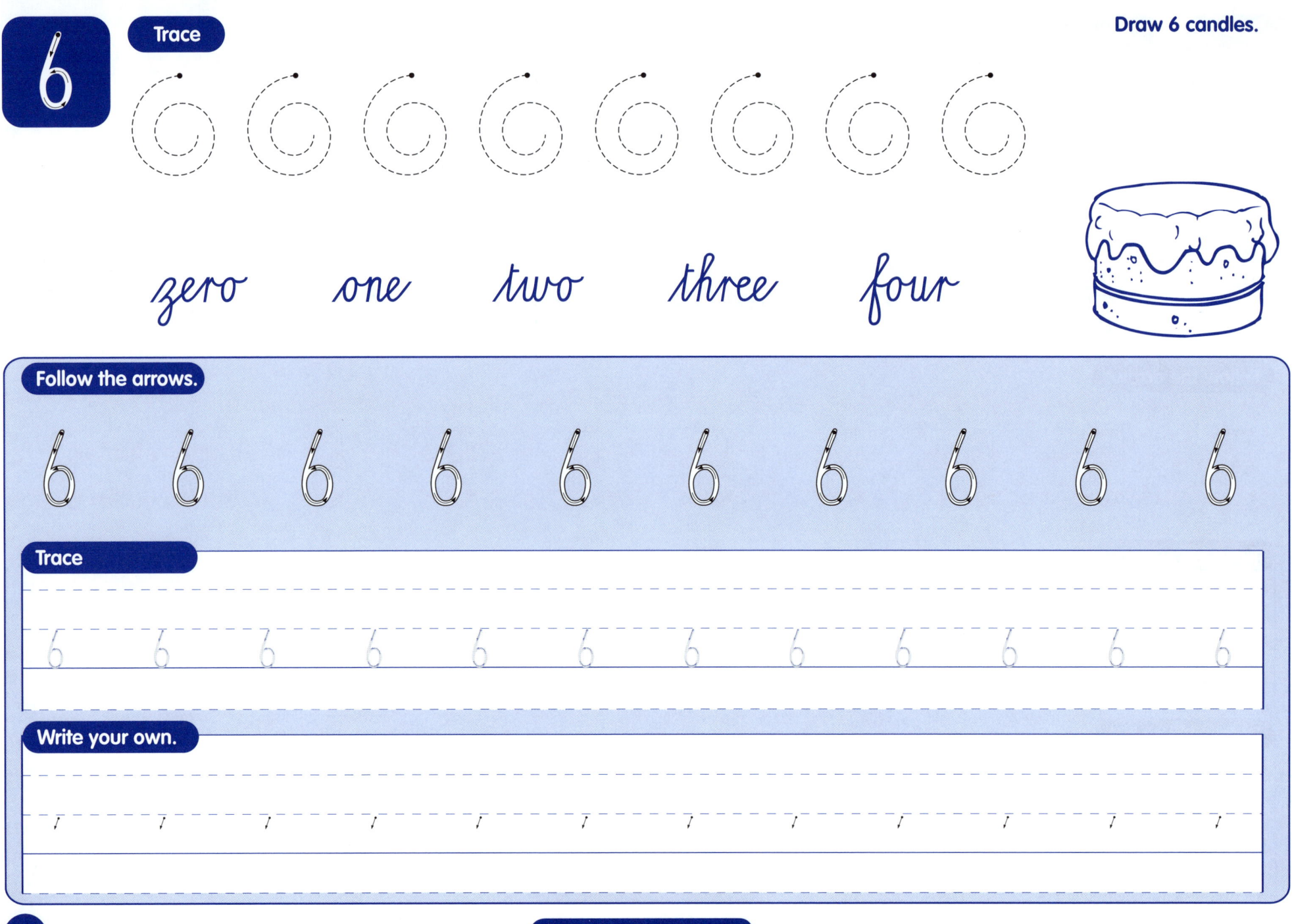

Handwriting Today

Prim-Ed Publishing – www.prim-ed.com

7

Trace

Draw 7 candles.

five   six   seven   eight   nine

Follow the arrows.

Trace

Write your own.

Handwriting Today

8 **Trace**

Draw 8 candles.

zero   one   two   three   four

Follow the arrows.

8 8 8 8 8 8 8 8 8 8

Trace

8 8 8 8 8 8 8 8 8 8 8 8

Write your own.

q **Trace**

Draw 9 candles.

five   six   seven   eight   nine

Follow the arrows.

q q q q q q q q q q q

Trace

q q q q q q q q q q q q

Write your own.

Handwriting Today

73

Prim-Ed Publishing – www.prim-ed.com

Review: 0 1 2 3 4 5 6 7 8 9

Trace

Follow the arrows.

0 1 2 3 4 5 6 7 8 9

Trace

0 1 2 3 4 5 6 7 8 9

Write your own.

74 — Handwriting Today

Prim-Ed Publishing – www.prim-ed.com

Count the pictures and write the number.

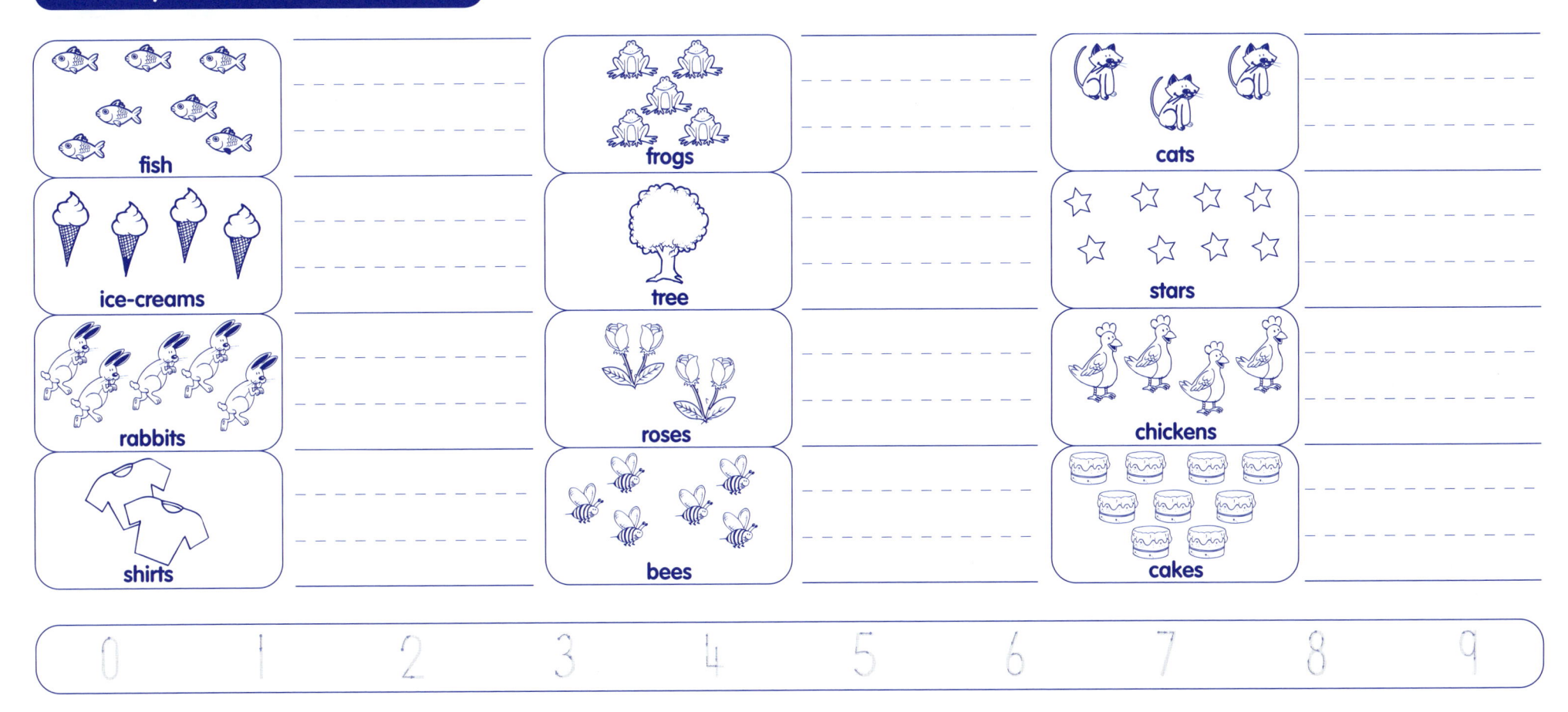

fish

ice-creams

rabbits

shirts

frogs

tree

roses

bees

cats

stars

chickens

cakes

0 1 2 3 4 5 6 7 8 9

Assessment	Demonstrated	Needs further opportunity		Demonstrated	Needs further opportunity	**General Comment**
• Uses a sharp pencil.			• Writes number words correctly.			
• Sits tall with both feet on the floor.			• Writes neatly and legibly.			
• Holds pencil correctly.			• Writes on the lines provided.			
• Forms numbers correctly.						

Handwriting Today

Prim-Ed Publishing – www.prim-ed.com

75

Assessment

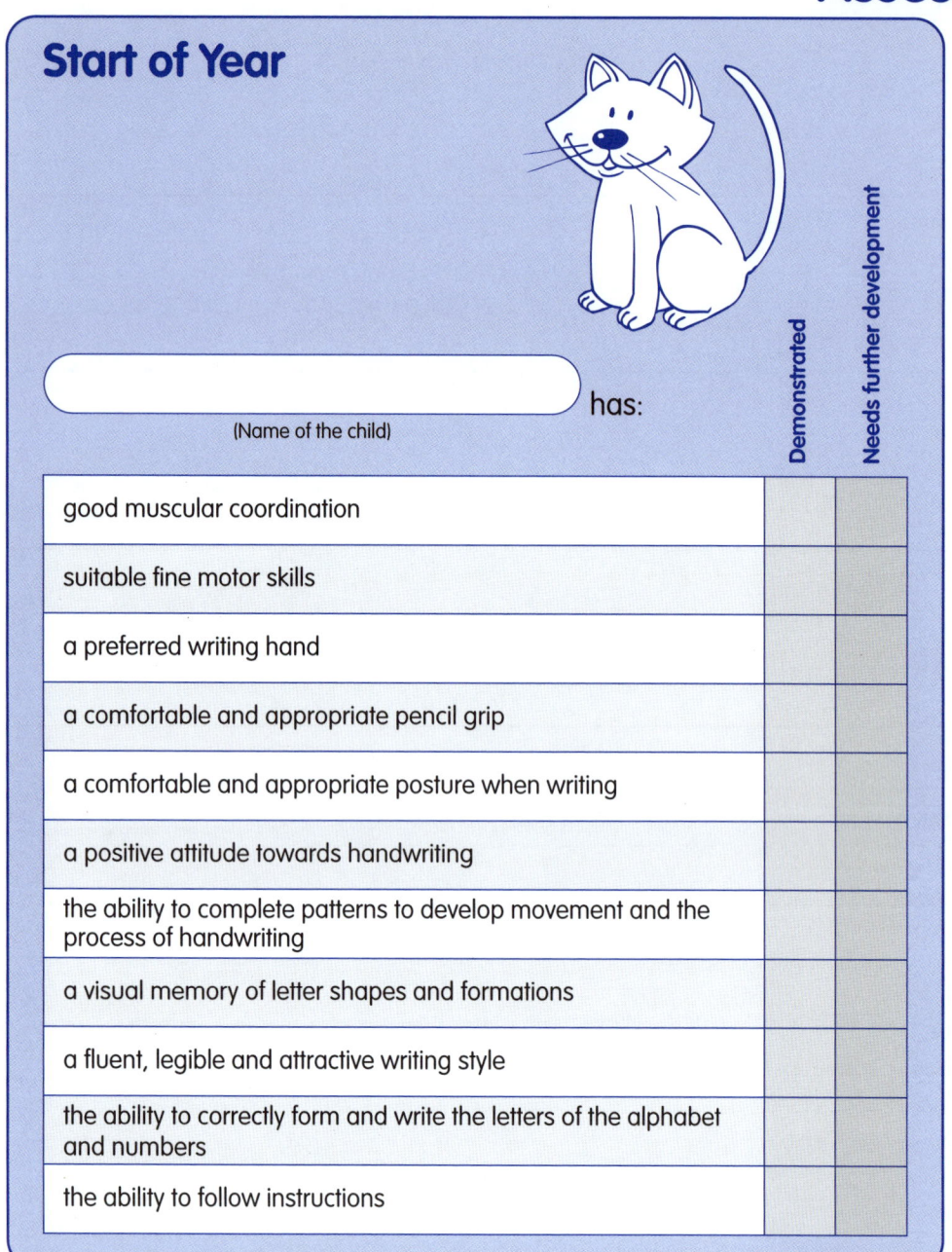

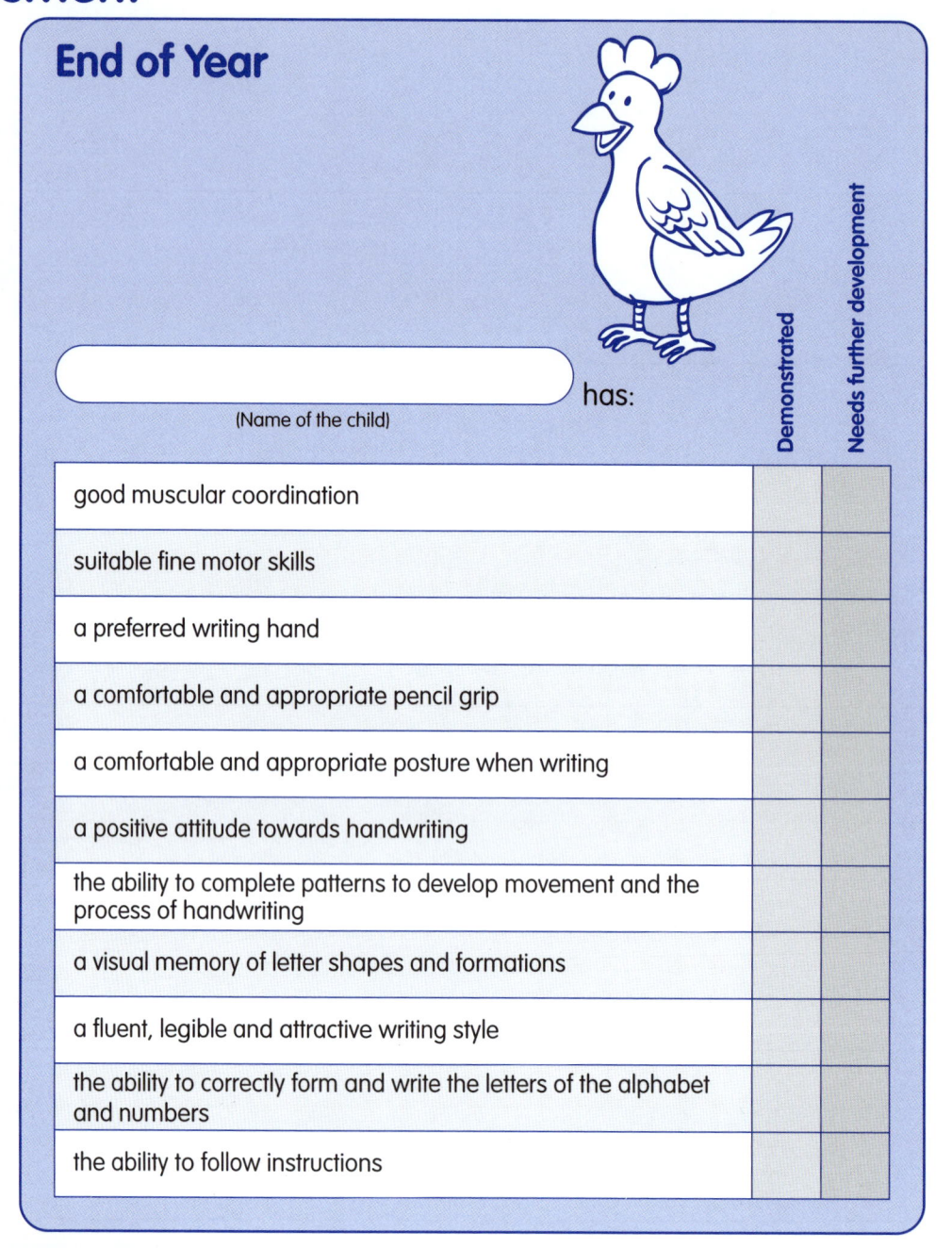

Start of Year

_____ has:
(Name of the child)

	Demonstrated	Needs further development
good muscular coordination		
suitable fine motor skills		
a preferred writing hand		
a comfortable and appropriate pencil grip		
a comfortable and appropriate posture when writing		
a positive attitude towards handwriting		
the ability to complete patterns to develop movement and the process of handwriting		
a visual memory of letter shapes and formations		
a fluent, legible and attractive writing style		
the ability to correctly form and write the letters of the alphabet and numbers		
the ability to follow instructions		

End of Year

_____ has:
(Name of the child)

	Demonstrated	Needs further development
good muscular coordination		
suitable fine motor skills		
a preferred writing hand		
a comfortable and appropriate pencil grip		
a comfortable and appropriate posture when writing		
a positive attitude towards handwriting		
the ability to complete patterns to develop movement and the process of handwriting		
a visual memory of letter shapes and formations		
a fluent, legible and attractive writing style		
the ability to correctly form and write the letters of the alphabet and numbers		
the ability to follow instructions		

Handwriting Today

Prim-Ed Publishing – www.prim-ed.com